BERLIN

THE WORLD 100 YEARS AGO

BERLIN

EGYPT

THE CITIES OF JAPAN

LONDON

MOSCOW

PARIS

PEKING

SOUTHERN ITALY

BURTON HOLMES

BERLIN

FRED L. ISRAEL
General Editor

ARTHUR M. SCHLESINGER, JR.
Senior Consulting Editor

CHELSEA HOUSE PUBLISHERS
Philadelphia

CHELSEA HOUSE PUBLISHERS

EDITOR-IN-CHIEF Stephen Reginald
MANAGING EDITOR James D. Gallagher
PRODUCTION MANAGER Pamela Loos
ART DIRECTOR Sara Davis
PICTURE EDITOR Judy Hasday
SENIOR PRODUCTION EDITOR Lisa Chippendale
ASSOCIATE ART DIRECTOR Takeshi Takahashi
COVER DESIGN Dave Loose Design

First Printing

1 3 5 7 9 8 6 4 2

Library of Congress Cataloging-in-Publication Data

Holmes, Burton, b. 1870.
Berlin/ by Burton Holmes; Fred L. Israel, general editor; Arthur M. Schlesinger, jr., senior consulting editor.
     p. cm. —(World 100 years ago)
Includes bibliographical references and index.

ISBN 0-7910-4664-8 (hc) ISBN 0-7910-4665-6 (pb).

1. Berlin (Germany)—Description and travel. 2. Berlin (Germany)—Social life and customs. 3. Travelers—History—Germany—Berlin—19th century. I. Israel, Fred L. II. Schlesinger, Arthur Meier, 1917- . III. Title. IV. Series: Holmes, Burton, b. 1870. World 100 years ago today.
DD860.H63   1997
914.3'1550484—dc21   97-31391
                                                              CIP

CONTENTS

THE GREAT GLOBE TROTTER

By Irving Wallace

One day in the year 1890, Miss Nellie Bly, of the *New York World,* came roaring into Brooklyn on a special train from San Francisco. In a successful effort to beat Phileas Fogg's fictional 80 days around the world, Miss Bly, traveling with two handbags and flannel underwear, had circled the globe in 72 days, 6 hours, and 11 minutes. Immortality awaited her.

Elsewhere that same year, another less-publicized globe-girdler made his start toward immortality. He was Mr. Burton Holmes, making his public debut with slides and anecdotes ("Through Europe With a Kodak") before the Chicago Camera Club. Mr. Holmes, while less spectacular than his feminine rival, was destined, for that very reason, soon to dethrone her as America's number-one traveler.

Today, Miss Bly and Mr. Holmes have one thing in common: In the mass mind they are legendary vagabonds relegated to the dim and dusty past of the Iron Horse and the paddle-wheel steamer. But if Miss Bly, who shuffled off this mortal coil in 1922, is now only a part of our folklore, there are millions to testify that

Mr. Burton Holmes, aged seventy-six, is still very much with us.

Remembering that Mr. Holmes was an active contemporary of Miss Bly's, that he was making a livelihood at traveling when William McKinley, John L. Sullivan, and Admiral Dewey ruled the United States, when Tony Pastor, Lily Langtry, and Lillian Russell ruled the amusement world, it is at once amazing and reassuring to pick up the daily newspapers of 1946 and find, sandwiched between advertisements of rash young men lecturing on "Inside Stalin" and "I Was Hitler's Dentist," calm announcements that tomorrow evening Mr. Burton Holmes has something more to say about "Beautiful Bali."

Burton Holmes, a brisk, immaculate, chunky man with gray Vandyke beard, erect bearing, precise speech ("folks are always mistaking me for Monty Woolley," he says, not unhappily), is one of the seven wonders of the entertainment world. As Everyman's tourist, Burton Holmes has crossed the Atlantic Ocean thirty times, the Pacific Ocean twenty times, and has gone completely around the world six times. He has spent fifty-five summers abroad, and recorded a half million feet of film of those summers. He was the first person to take motion picture cameras into Russia and Japan. He witnessed the regular decennial performance of the Passion Play at Oberammergau in 1890, and attended the first modern Olympics at Athens in 1896. He rode on the first Trans-Siberian train across Russia, and photographed the world's first airplane meet at Rheims.

As the fruit of these travels, Burton Holmes has delivered approximately 8,000 illustrated lectures that have grossed, according to an estimate by *Variety,* five million dollars in fifty-three winters. Because he does not like to be called a lecturer— "I'm a performer," he insists, "and I have performed on more legitimate stages than platforms"—he invented the word "travelogue" in London to describe his activity.

His travelogues, regarded as a fifth season of the year in most communities, have won him such popularity that he holds the record for playing in the longest one-man run in American show business. In the five and a half decades past, Burton Holmes has successively met the hectic competition of big-time vaudeville, stage, silent pictures, radio, and talking pictures, and he has survived them all.

At an age when most men have retired to slippered ease or are hounded by high blood pressure, Burton Holmes is more active and more popular than ever before. In the season just finished, which he started in San Francisco during September, 1945, and wound up in New York during April, 1946, Holmes appeared in 187 shows, a record number. He averaged six travelogues a week, spoke for two hours at each, and did 30 percent more box-office business than five years ago. Not once was a scheduled lecture postponed or canceled. In fact, he has missed only two in his life. In 1935, flying over the Dust Bowl, he suffered laryngitis and was forced to bypass two college dates. He has never canceled an appearance before a paid city audience. Seven years ago, when one of his elderly limbs was fractured in an automobile crack-up in Finland, there was a feeling that Burton Holmes might not make the rounds. When news of the accident was released, it was as if word had gone out that Santa Claus was about to cancel his winter schedule. But when the 1939 season dawned, Burton Holmes rolled on the stage in a wheelchair, and from his seat of pain (and for 129 consecutive appearances thereafter), he delivered his travel chat while 16-mm film shimmered on the screen beside him.

Today, there is little likelihood that anything, except utter extinction, could keep Holmes from his waiting audiences. Even now, between seasons, Holmes is in training for his next series— 150 illustrated lectures before groups in seventeen states.

Before World War II, accompanied by Margaret Oliver, his wife of thirty-two years, Holmes would spend his breathing spells on summery excursions through the Far East or Europe. While aides captured scenery on celluloid, Holmes wrote accompanying lecture material in his notebooks. Months later, he would communicate his findings to his cult, at a maximum price of $1.50 per seat. With the outbreak of war, Holmes changed his pattern. He curtailed travel outside the Americas. This year, except for one journey to Las Vegas, Nevada, where he personally photographed cowboy cutups and shapely starlets at the annual Helldorado festival, Holmes has been allowing his assistants to do all his traveling for him.

Recently, one crew, under cameraman Thayer Soule, who helped shoot the Battle of Tarawa for the Marines, brought Holmes a harvest of new film from Mexico. Another crew, after four months in Brazil last year, and two in its capital this year, returned to Holmes with magnificent movies. Meantime, other crews, under assignment from Holmes, are finishing films on Death Valley, the West Indies, and the Mississippi River.

In a cottage behind his sprawling Hollywood hilltop home, Holmes is busy, day and night, sorting the incoming negative, cutting and editing it, and rewriting lectures that will accompany the footage this winter. He is too busy to plan his next trip. Moreover, he doesn't feel that he should revisit Europe yet. "I wouldn't mind seeing it," he says, "but I don't think my public would be interested. My people want a good time, they want escape, they want sweetness and light, beauty and charm. There is too much rubble and misery over there now, and I'll let those picture magazines and Fox Movietone newsreels show all that. I'll wait until it's tourist time again."

When he travels, he thinks he will visit three of the four accessible places on earth that he has not yet seen. One is Tahiti, which he barely missed a dozen times, and the other two are Iran and Iraq. The remaining country that he has not seen, and has no wish to see, is primitive Afghanistan. Of all cities on earth, he would most like to revisit Kyoto, once capital of Japan. He still recalls that the first movies ever made inside Japan were ones he made in Kyoto, in 1899. The other cities he desires to revisit are

Venice and Rome. The only island for which he has any longing is Bali—"the one quaint spot on earth where you can really get away from it all."

In preparing future subjects, Holmes carefully studies the success of his past performances. Last season, his two most popular lectures in the East were "California" and "Adventures in Mexico." The former grossed $5,100 in two Chicago shows; the latter jammed the St. Louis Civic Auditorium with thirty-five hundred potential señores and señoritas. Holmes will use these subjects again, with revisions, next season, and add some brand-new Latin American and United States topics. He will sidestep anything relating to war. He feels, for example, that anything dealing with the once exotic Pacific islands might have a questionable reception—"people will still remember those white crosses they saw in newsreels of Guadalcanal and Iwo Jima."

Every season presents its own obstacles, and the next will challenge Holmes with a new audience of travel-sated and disillusioned ex-GI's. Many of these men, and their families, now know that a South Sea island paradise means mosquitoes and malaria and not Melville's Fayaway and Loti's Rarahu. They know Europe means mud and ruins and not romance. Nevertheless, Holmes is confident that he will win these people over.

"The veterans of World War II will come to my travelogues just as their fathers did. After the First World War, I gave illustrated lectures on the sights of France, and the ex-doughboys enjoyed them immensely. But I suppose there's no use comparing that war to this. The First World War was a minor dispute between gentlemen. In this one, the atrocities and miseries will be difficult to forget. I know I can't give my Beautiful Italy lecture next season to men who know Italy only as a pigsty, but you see, in my heart Italy is forever beautiful, and I see things in Italy they can't see, poor fellows. How could they? . . . Still, memory is frail, and one day these boys will forget and come to my lectures not to hoot but to relive the better moments and enjoy themselves."

While Burton Holmes prepares his forthcoming shows, his business manager, a slightly built dynamo named Walter Everest, works on next season's bookings. Everest contacts organizations interested in sponsoring a lecture series, arranges dates and prices, and often leases auditoriums on his own. Everest concentrates on cities where Holmes is known to be popular, Standing Room Only cities like New York, Boston, Philadelphia, Chicago, Los Angeles. On the other hand, he is cautious about the cities where Holmes has been unpopular in the past—Toledo, Cleveland, Indianapolis, Cincinnati. The one city Holmes now avoids entirely is Pomona, California, where, at a scheduled Saturday matinee, he found himself facing an almost empty house. The phenomenon of a good city or a poor city is inexplicable. In rare cases, there may be a reason for failure, and then Holmes will attempt to resolve it. When San Francisco was stone-deaf to Holmes, investigation showed that he had been competing with the annual opera season. Last year, he rented a theater the week before the opera began. He appeared eight times and made a handsome profit.

Once Holmes takes to the road for his regular season, he is a perpetual-motion machine. Leaving his wife behind, he barnstorms with his manager, Everest, and a projectionist, whirling to Western dates in his Cadillac, making long hops by plane, following the heavier Eastern circuit by train. Holmes likes to amaze younger men with his activities during a typical week. If he speaks in Detroit on a Tuesday night, he will lecture in Chicago on Wednesday evening, in Milwaukee on Thursday, be back in Chicago for Friday evening and a Saturday matinee session, then go on to Kansas City on Sunday, St. Louis on Monday, and play a return engagement in Detroit on Tuesday.

This relentless merry-go-round (with Saturday nights off to attend a newsreel "and see what's happening in the world") invigorates Holmes, but grinds his colleagues to a frazzle. One morning last season, after weeks of trains and travel, Walter

Everest was awakened by a porter at six. He rose groggily, sat swaying on the edge of his berth trying to put on his shoes. He had the look of a man who had pushed through the Matto Grosso on foot. He glanced up sleepily, and there, across the aisle, was Holmes, fully dressed, looking natty and refreshed. Holmes smiled sympathetically. "I know, Walter," he said, "this life is tiring. One day both of us ought to climb on some train and get away from it all."

In his years on the road, Holmes has come to know his audience thoroughly. He is firm in the belief that it is composed mostly of traveled persons who wish to savor the glamorous sights of the world again. Through Burton, they relive their own tours. Of the others, some regard a Holmes performance as a preview. They expect to travel; they want to know the choice sights for their future three-month jaunt to Ecuador. Some few, who consider themselves travel authorities, come to a Holmes lecture to point out gleefully the good things that he missed. "It makes them happy," Holmes says cheerfully. Tomorrow's audience, for the most, will be the same as the one that heard the Master exactly a year before. Generations of audiences inherit Holmes, one from the other.

An average Holmes lecture combines the atmosphere of a revival meeting and a family get-together at which home movies are shown. A typical Holmes travelogue begins in a brightly lit auditorium, at precisely three minutes after eight-thirty. The three minutes is to allow for latecomers. Holmes, attired in formal evening clothes, strides from the wings to center stage. People applaud; some cheer. Everyone seems to know him and to know exactly what to expect. Holmes smiles broadly. He is compact, proper, handsome. His goatee dominates the scene. He has worn it every season, with the exception of one in 1895 (when, beardless, he somewhat resembled Paget's Sherlock Holmes). Now, he speaks crisply. He announces that this is the third lecture of his fifty-fourth season. He announces his subject—"Adventures in Mexico."

He walks to one side of the stage, where a microphone is standing. The lights are dimmed. The auditorium becomes dark. Beyond the fifth row, Holmes cannot be seen. The all-color 16-mm film is projected on the screen. The film opens, minus title and credits, with a shot through the windshield of an automobile speeding down the Pan-American Highway to Monterrey. Holmes himself is the sound track. His speech, with just the hint of a theatrical accent, is intimate, as if he were talking in a living room. He punctuates descriptive passages with little formal jokes. When flowers and orange trees of Mexico are on the screen, he says, "We have movies and talkies, but now we should have smellies and tasties"—and he chuckles.

The film that he verbally captions is a dazzling, uncritical montage of Things Mexican. There is a señora selling tortillas, and close-ups of how tortillas are made. There is a bullfight, but not the kill. There is snow-capped Popocatepetl, now for sale at the bargain price of fifteen million dollars. There are the pyramids outside Mexico City, older than those of Egypt, built by the ancient Toltecs who went to war with wooden swords so that they would not kill their enemies.

Holmes's movies and lectures last two hours, with one intermission. The emphasis is on description, information, and oddity. Two potential ingredients are studiously omitted. One is adventure, the other politics. Holmes is never spectacular. "I want nothing dangerous. I don't care to emulate the explorers, to risk my neck, to be the only one or the first one there. Let others tackle the Himalayas, the Amazon, the North Pole, let them break the trails for me. I'm just a Cook's tourist, a little ahead of the crowd, but not too far ahead." Some years ago, Holmes did think that he was an explorer, and became very excited about it, he now admits sheepishly. This occurred in a trackless sector of Northern Rhodesia. Holmes felt that he had discovered a site never before seen by an outsider. Grandly, he planted the flag of the Explorers

Club, carefully he set up his camera, and then, as he prepared to shoot, his glance fell upon an object several feet away—an empty Kodak carton. Quietly, he repacked and stole away—and has stayed firmly on the beaten paths ever since.

As to politics, it never taints his lectures. He insists neither he nor his audiences are interested. "When you discuss politics," he says, "you are sure to offend." Even after his third trip to Russia, he refused to discuss politics. "I am a traveler," he explained at that time, "and not a student of political and economic questions. To me, Communism is merely one of the sights I went to see."

However, friends know that Holmes has his pet panacea for the ills of the world. He is violent about the gold standard, insisting that it alone can make all the world prosperous. Occasionally, when the mood is on him, and against his better judgment, he will inject propaganda in favor of the gold standard into an otherwise timid travelogue.

When he is feeling mellow, Holmes will confess that once in the past he permitted politics to intrude upon his sterile chitchat. It was two decades ago, when he jousted with Prohibition. While not a dedicated drinking man, Holmes has been on a friendly basis with firewater since the age of sixteen. In the ensuing years, he has regularly, every dusk before dinner, mixed himself one or two highballs. Only once did he try more than two, and the results were disastrous. "Any man who drinks three will drink three hundred," he now says righteously. Holmes felt that Prohibition was an insult to civilized living. As a consequence of this belief, his audiences during the days of the Eighteenth Amendment were often startled to hear Holmes extol the virtues of open drinking, in the middle of a placid discourse on Oberammergau or Lapland. "Sometimes an indignant female would return her tickets to the rest of my series," he says, "but there were others, more intelligent, to take her place."

This independent attitude in Holmes was solely the product of his personal success. Born in January, 1870, of a financially secure, completely cosmopolitan Chicago family, he was able to be independent from his earliest days. His father, an employee in the Third National Bank, distinguished himself largely by lending George Pullman enough cash to transform his old day coaches into the first Pullman Palace Sleeping Cars, and by refusing a half interest in the business in exchange for his help. Even to this day, it makes Burton Holmes dizzy to think of the money he might have saved in charges for Pullman berths.

Holmes's interest in show business began at the age of nine when his grandmother, Ann W. Burton, took him to hear John L. Stoddard lecture on the Passion Play at Oberammergau. Young Holmes was never the same again. After brief visits to faraway Florida and California, he quit school and accompanied his grandmother on his first trip abroad. He was sixteen and wide-eyed. His grandmother, who had traveled with her wine-salesman husband to France and Egypt and down the Volga in the sixties, was the perfect guide. But this journey through Europe was eclipsed, four years later, by a more important pilgrimage with his grandmother to Germany. The first day at his hotel in Munich, Holmes saw John L. Stoddard pass through the lobby reading a Baedeker. He was petrified. It was as if he had seen his Maker. Even now, over a half century later, when Holmes speaks about Stoddard, his voice carries a tinge of awe. For eighteen years of the later nineteenth century, Stoddard, with black-and-white slides and magnificent oratory, dominated the travel-lecture field. To audiences, young and old, he was the most romantic figure in America. Later, at Oberammergau, Holmes sat next to Stoddard through the fifteen acts of the Passion Play and they became friends.

When Holmes returned to the States, some months after Nellie Bly had made her own triumphal return to Brooklyn, he showed rare Kodak negatives of his travels to fellow members of the Chicago Camera Club. The members were impressed, and one suggested that these be mounted as slides and shown to the general public. "To take the edge off the silence, to keep the show moving," says Holmes, "I wrote an account of my journey and read it, as the stereopticon man changed slides." The show, which grossed the club $350, was Holmes's initial travelogue. However, he dates the beginning of his professional career from three years later, when he appeared under his own auspices with hand-colored slides.

After the Camera Club debut, Holmes did not go immediately into the travelogue field. He was not yet ready to appreciate its possibilities. Instead, he attempted to sell real estate, and failed. Then he worked for eight dollars a week as a photo supply clerk. In 1902, aching with wanderlust, he bullied his family into staking him to a five-month tour of Japan. On the boat he was thrilled to find John L. Stoddard, also bound for Japan. They became closer friends, even though they saw Nippon through different eyes. "The older man found Japan queer, quaint, comfortless, and almost repellent," Stoddard's son wrote years later. "To the younger man it was a fairyland." Stoddard invited Holmes to continue on around the world with him, but Holmes loved Japan and decided to remain.

When Holmes returned to Chicago, the World's Columbian Exposition of 1893 was in full swing. He spent months at the Jackson Park grounds, under Edison's new electric lights, listening to Lillian Russell sing, Susan B. Anthony speak, and watching Sandow perform feats of strength. With rising excitement, he observed Jim Brady eating, Anthony Comstock snorting at Little Egypt's hootchy-kootchy, and Alexander Dowie announcing himself as the Prophet Elijah III.

In the midst of this excitement came the depression of that year. Holmes's father suffered. "He hit the wheat pit at the wrong time, and I had to go out on my own," says Holmes. "The photo supply house offered me fifteen dollars a week to return. But I didn't want to work. The trip to Japan, the Oriental exhibits of the Exposition, were still on my mind. I thought of

Stoddard. I thought of the slides I'd had hand-colored in Tokyo. That was it, and it wasn't work. So I hired a hall and became a travel lecturer."

Copying society addresses from his mother's visiting list, and additional addresses from *The Blue Book,* Holmes mailed two thousand invitations in the form of Japanese poem-cards. Recipients were invited to two illustrated lectures, at $1.50 each, on "Japan—the Country and the Cities." Both performances were sellouts. Holmes grossed $700.

For four years Holmes continued his fight to win a steady following, but with only erratic success. Then, in 1897, when he stood at the brink of defeat, two events occurred to change his life. First, John L. Stoddard retired from the travel-lecture field and threw the platforms of the nation open to a successor. Second, Holmes supplemented colored slides with a new method of illustrating his talks. As his circular announced, "There will be presented for the first time in connection with a course of travel lectures a series of pictures to which a modern miracle has added the illusion of life itself—the reproduction of recorded motion."

Armed with his jumpy movies—scenes of the Omaha fire department, a police parade in Chicago, Italians eating spaghetti, each reel running twenty-five seconds, with a four-minute wait between reels—Burton Holmes invaded the Stoddard strongholds in the East. Stoddard came to hear him and observe the newfangled movies. Like Marshal Foch who regarded the airplane as "an impractical toy," Stoddard saw no future in the motion picture. Nevertheless, he gave young Holmes a hand by insisting that Augustin Daly lease his Manhattan theater to the newcomer. This done, Stoddard retired to the Austrian Tyrol, and Holmes went on to absorb Stoddard's audiences in Boston and Philadelphia and to win new followers of his own throughout the nation.

His success assured, Holmes began to gather material with a vigor that was to make him one of history's most indefatigable travelers. In 1900, at the Paris Exposition, sitting in a restaurant built like a Russian train, drinking vodka while a colored panorama of Siberia rolled past his window, he succumbed to this unique advertising of the new Trans-Siberian railway and bought a ticket. The trip in 1901 was a nightmare. After ten days on the Trans-Siberian train, which banged along at eleven miles an hour, Holmes was dumped into a construction train for five days, and then spent twenty-seven days on steamers going down the Amur River. It took him forty-two and a half days to travel from Moscow to Vladivostok.

But during that tour, he had one great moment. He saw Count Leo Tolstoi at Yasnaya Polyana, the author's country estate near Tula. At a dinner in Moscow, Holmes met Albert J. Beveridge, the handsome senator from Indiana. Beveridge had a letter of introduction to Tolstoi and invited Holmes and his enormous 60-mm movie camera to come along. Arriving in a four-horse landau, the Americans were surprised to find Tolstoi's house dilapidated. Then, they were kept waiting two hours. At last, the seventy-three-year-old, white-bearded Tolstoi, nine years away from his lonely death in a railway depot, appeared. He was attired in a mujik costume. He invited his visitors to breakfast, then conversed in fluent English. "He had only a slight accent, and he spoke with the cadence of Sir Henry Irving," Holmes recalls.

Of the entire morning's conversation, Holmes remembers clearly only one remark. That was when Tolstoi harangued, "There should be no law. No man should have the right to judge or condemn another. Absolute freedom of the individual is the only thing that can redeem the world. Christ was a great teacher, nothing more!" As Tolstoi continued to speak, Holmes quietly set up his movie camera. Tolstoi had never seen one before. He posed stiffly, as for a daguerreotype. When he thought that it was over, and resumed his talking, Holmes began actual shooting. This priceless film never reached the screen. Senator Beveridge was then a presidential possibility. His managers feared that this film of Beveridge with a Russian radical might be used by his opponents. The film was taken from Holmes and destroyed. Later, when he was not even nominated for the presidency, Beveridge wrote an apology to Holmes, "for this destruction of so valuable a living record of the grand old Russian."

In 1934, at a cost of ten dollars a day, Holmes spent twenty-one days in modern Soviet Russia. He loved the ballet, the omelets, the Russian rule against tipping, and the lack of holdups. He went twice to see the embalmed Lenin, fascinated by the sight of "his head resting on a red pillow like that of a tired man asleep."

Although Holmes's name had already appeared on eighteen travel volumes, this last Russian trip inspired him to write his first and only original book. The earlier eighteen volumes, all heavily illustrated, were offered as a set, of which over forty thousand were sold. However, they were not "written," but were actually a collection of lectures delivered orally by Holmes. The one book that he wrote as a book, *The Traveler's Russia,* published in 1934 by G.P. Putnam's Sons, was a failure. Holmes has bought the remainders and passes them out to guests with a variety of inscriptions. In a serious mood he will inscribe, "To travel is to possess the world." In a frivolous mood, he will write "With love from Tovarich Burtonovich Holmeski."

In the five decades past, Holmes has kept himself occupied with a wide variety of pleasures, such as attending Queen Victoria's Golden Jubilee in London, chatting with Admiral Dewey in Hong Kong, driving the first automobile seen in Denmark, and photographing a mighty eruption of Vesuvius.

In 1918, wearing a war correspondent's uniform, he shot army scenes on the Western Front and his films surpassed those of the poorly organized newsreel cameramen. In 1923, flying for the first time, he had his most dangerous experience, when his plane almost crashed between Toulouse and Rabat. Later, in

Berlin, he found his dollar worth ten million marks, and in Africa he interviewed Emperor Haile Selassie in French, and, closer to home, he flew 20,000 miles over Central and South America.

Burton Holmes enjoys company on his trips. By coincidence, they are often celebrities. Holmes traveled through Austria with Maria Jeritza, through Greece with E.F. Benson, through the Philippines with Dr. Victor Heiser. He covered World War I with Harry Franck, wandered about Japan with Lafcadio Hearn's son, crossed Ethiopia with the Duke of Gloucester. He saw Hollywood with Mary Pickford, Red Square with Alma Gluck, and the Andes with John McCutcheon.

Of the hundreds of travelogues that Holmes has delivered, the most popular was "The Panama Canal." He offered this in 1912, when the "big ditch" was under construction, and news-hungry citizens flocked to hear him. Among less timely subjects, his most popular was the standard masterpiece on Oberammergau, followed closely by his illustrated lectures on the "Frivolities of Paris," the "Canals of Venice," the "Countryside of England" and, more currently, "Adventures in Mexico." Burton Holmes admits that his greatest failure was an elaborate travelogue on Siam, even though it seemed to have everything except Anna and the King thereof. Other failures included travelogues on India, Burma, Ethiopia, and—curiously—exotic Bali. The only two domestic subjects to fizzle were "Down in Dixie" in 1915 and "The Century of Progress Exposition" in 1932.

All in all, the success of Holmes's subjects has been so consistently high that he has never suffered seriously from competition. One rival died, another retired eight years ago. "I'm the lone survivor of the magic-lantern boys," says Holmes. Of the younger crowd, Holmes thought that Richard Halliburton might become his successor. "He deserved to carry the banner," says Holmes. "He was good-looking, with a fine classical background, intelligent, interesting, and he really did those darn-fool stunts." Halliburton, who had climbed the Matterhorn, swum the Hellespont, followed the Cortés train through Mexico, lectured with slides. "I told him to throw away the slides," says Holmes. "He was better without them, his speech was so colorful." When Halliburton died attempting to sail a Chinese junk across the Pacific, Holmes decided to present an illustrated lecture on "The Romantic Adventures of Richard Halliburton." He used his own movies but, in the accompanying talk, Halliburton's written text. "It was a crashing failure," sighs Holmes. "His millions of fans did not want to hear me, and my fans did not want to know about him."

For a while, Hollywood appeared to be the travelogue's greatest threat. Holmes defeated this menace by marriage with the studios. He signed a contract with Paramount, made fifty-two travel shorts each year, between 1915 and 1921. Then, with the advent of talking pictures, Holmes joined Metro-Goldwyn-Mayer and made a series of travelogues, released in English, French, Italian, Spanish. In 1933, he made his debut in radio, and in 1944 made his first appearance on television.

Today, safe in the knowledge that he is an institution, Holmes spends more and more time in his rambling, plantation-style, wooden home, called "Topside," located on a hill a mile above crowded Hollywood Boulevard. This dozen-roomed brown house, once a riding club for silent day film stars, and owned for six years by Francis X. Bushman (who gave it Hollywood's first swimming pool, where Holmes now permits neighborhood children to splash), was purchased by Holmes in 1930. "I had that M-G-M contract," he says, "and it earned me a couple of hundred thousand dollars. Well, everyone with a studio contract immediately gets himself a big car, a big house, and a small blonde. I acquired the car, the house, but kept the blonde a mental acquisition." For years, Holmes also owned a Manhattan duplex decorated with costly Japanese and Buddhist treasures, which he called "Nirvana." Before Pearl Harbor, Holmes sold the duplex, with its two-million-dollar collection of furnishings, to Robert Ripley, the cartoonist and oddity hunter.

Now, in his rare moments of leisure, Holmes likes to sit on the veranda of his Hollywood home and chat with his wife. Before he met her, he had been involved in one public romance. Gossips, everywhere, insisted that he might marry the fabulous Elsie de Wolfe, actress, millionaire decorator, friend of Oscar Wilde and Sarah Bernhardt, who later became Lady Mendl. Once, in Denver, Holmes recalls, a reporter asked him if he was engaged to Elsie de Wolfe. Holmes replied, curtly, No. That afternoon a banner headline proclaimed: BURTON HOLMES REFUSES TO MARRY ELSIE DE WOLFE!

Shortly afterward, during a photographic excursion, Holmes met Margaret Oliver who, suffering from deafness, had taken up still photography as an avocation. In 1914, following a moonlight proposal on a steamer's deck, he married Miss Oliver in New York City's St. Stephen's Episcopal Church, and took her to prosaic Atlantic City for the first few days of their honeymoon, then immediately embarked on a long trip abroad.

When his wife is out shopping, Holmes will stroll about his estate, study his fifty-four towering palm trees, return to the veranda for a highball, thumb through the *National Geographic,* play with his cats, or pick up a language textbook. He is on speaking terms with eight languages, including some of the Scandinavian, and is eager to learn more. He never reads travel books. "As Pierre Loti once remarked, 'I don't read. It might ruin my style,'" he explains.

He likes visitors, and he will startle them with allusions to his earlier contemporaries. "This lawn part reminds me of the one at which I met Emperor Meiji," he will say. Meiji, grandfather of Hirohito, opened Japan to Commodore Perry. When visitors ask for his travel advice, Holmes invariably tells them to see the Americas first. "Why go to Mont St. Michel?" he asks. "Have you seen Monticello?"

But when alone with his wife and co-workers on the veranda,

and the pressure of the new season is weeks away, he will loosen his blue dressing gown, inhale, then stare reflectively out over the sun-bathed city below.

"You know, this is the best," he will say softly, "looking down on this Los Angeles. It is heaven. I could sit here the rest of my life." Then, suddenly, he will add, "There is so much else to see and do. If only I could have another threescore years upon this planet. If only I could know the good earth better than I do."

Note: Irving Wallace (1916-1990) wrote this article on the occasion of Burton Holmes's 77th birthday. It was originally printed in *The Saturday Evening Post* May 10, 1947. Holmes retired the following year from presenting his travelogues in person. He died in 1958 at age 88. His autobiography, *The World is Mine,* was published in 1953.

Reprinted by permission of Mrs. Sylvia Wallace.

Burton Holmes

By Arthur M. Schlesinger, jr.

B urton Holmes!—forgotten today, but such a familiar name in America in the first half of the 20th century, a name then almost synonymous with dreams of foreign travel. In the era before television brought the big world into the households of America, it was Burton Holmes who brought the world to millions of Americans in crowded lecture halls, and did so indefatigably for 60 years. I still remember going with my mother in the 1920s to Symphony Hall in Boston, watching the brisk, compact man with a Vandyke beard show his films of Venice or Bali or Kyoto and describe foreign lands in engaging and affectionate commentary.

Burton Holmes invented the word "travelogue" in 1904. He embodied it for the rest of his life. He was born in Chicago in 1870 and made his first trip abroad at the age of 16. Taking a camera along on his second trip, he mounted his black-and-white negatives on slides and showed them to friends in the Chicago Camera Club. "To keep the show moving," he said later, "I wrote an account of my journey and read it, as the stereopticon man changed slides." He had discovered his métier. Soon he had his slides hand-colored and was in business as a professional lecturer. In time, as technology developed, slides gave way to moving pictures.

Holmes was a tireless traveler, forever ebullient and optimistic, uninterested in politics and poverty and the darker side of life, in love with beautiful scenery, historic monuments, picturesque customs, and challenging trips. He was there at the Athens Olympics in 1896, at the opening of the Trans-Siberian railway, at the Passion Play in Oberammergau. His popular lectures had such titles as "The Magic of Mexico," "The Canals of Venice," "The Glories and Frivolities of Paris." His illustrated travel books enthralled thousands of American families. He also filmed a series of travelogues—silent pictures for Paramount, talkies for Metro-Goldwyn-Mayer.

He wanted his fellow countrymen to rejoice in the wonders of the great globe. "I'm a Cook's tourist," he said, referring to the famous tours conducted by Thomas Cook and Sons, "reporting how pleasant it is in such and such a place." He knew that the world was less than perfect, but he thought the worst sufficiently documented, and his mission, as he saw it, was to bring people the best. Reflecting at the end of the Second World War on the mood of returning veterans, he said, "The atrocities and miseries will be difficult to forget. I know I can't give my Beautiful Italy lecture next session to men who know Italy only as a pigsty . . . One day these boys will forget and come to my lectures not to hoot but to relive the better moments and enjoy themselves."

When he retired in 1951, Burton Holmes had delivered over 8,000 lectures. By the time he died in 1958, television had taken over the job he had discharged so ardently for more than half a century. He taught generations of Americans about the great world beyond the seas. His books are still readable today and show new generations how their grandparents learned about a world that has since passed away but remains a fragrant memory.

THE WORLD 100 YEARS AGO

By Dr. Fred Israel

The generation that lived 100 years ago was the first to leave behind a comprehensive visual record. It was the camera that made this possible. The great photographers of the 1860s and 1870s took their unwieldy equipment to once-unimaginable places—from the backstreets of London to the homesteads of the American frontier; from tribal Africa to the temples of Japan. They photographed almost the entire world.

Burton Holmes (1870-1958) ranks among the pioneers who popularized photojournalism. He had an insatiable curiosity. "There was for me the fascination of magic in photography," Holmes wrote. "The word Kodak had not yet been coined. You could not press the button and let someone else do the rest. You had to do it all yourself and know what you were doing." Holmes combined his love of photography with a passion for travel. It didn't really matter where—only that it be exciting.

"Shut your eyes, tight!" said Holmes. "Imagine the sands of the Sahara, the temples of Japan, the beach at Waikiki, the fjords of Norway, the vastness of Panama, the great gates of Peking." It was this type of visual imagination that made Burton Holmes America's best known travel lecturer. By his 75th birthday, he had crossed the Atlantic Ocean 30 times and the Pacific 20, and he had gone around the world on six occasions. Variety magazine estimated that in his five-decade career, Holmes had delivered more than 8,000 lectures describing almost every corner of the earth.

Burton Holmes was born in Chicago on January 8, 1870. His privileged background contributed to his lifelong fascination with travel. When he was 16, his maternal grandmother took him on a three-month European trip, about which he later wrote:

> I still recall our first meal ashore, the delicious English sole served at the Adelphi Hotel [Liverpool] . . . Edinburgh thrilled me, but Paris! I would gladly have travelled third class or on a bike or on foot. Paris at last! I knew my Paris in advance. Had I not studied the maps and plans? I knew I could find my way to Notre Dame and to the Invalides without asking anyone which way to go. (The Eiffel Tower had not yet been built.) From a bus-top, I surveyed the boulevards—recognizing all the famous sights. Then for a panoramic survey of the city, I climbed the towers of Notre Dame, then the Tour St. Jacques, the Bastille Column, and finally the Arc De Triomphe, all in one long day. That evening, I was in Montmartre, where as yet there stood no great domed church of the Sacre Coeur. But at the base of the famous hill were the red windmill wings of the Moulin Rouge revolving in all their majesty. My French—school French—was pretty bad but it sufficed. Paris was the springtime of my life!

Holmes never lost his passion for travel nor his passion for capturing his observations on film. He has left us with a unique and remarkable record that helps us to visualize the world many decades ago.

Lecturing became Holmes's profession. In 1892-93 he toured Japan. He discovered that "it was my native land in some previous incarnation—and the most beautiful land I have known." Holmes had the idea of giving an illustrated lecture about Japan to an affluent Chicago audience:

> I had brought home a large number of Japanese cards such as
> are used in Japan for sending poems or New Year's greetings.
> They were about two inches by fourteen inches long. I had the
> idea that they would, by their odd shape, attract instant notice.
> So I had envelopes made for them, employing a Japanese artist
> to make a design.

Holmes sent about 2,000 invitations to the socially prominent
whose addresses he took from the *Blue Book*. He "invited" them
to two illustrated lectures at $1.50 each on "Japan—the Country
and the Cities." ($1.50 was a high sum for the 1890s considering
that the average worker earned about $1 per day.) Both perfor-
mances sold out.

Burton Holmes's "Travelogues" (he began using the term in
1904) rapidly became part of American upper class societal life.
Holmes engaged the best theater or concert hall for a week at a
time. His appearance was an annual event at Carnegie Hall in
New York, Symphony Hall in Boston, and Orchestra Hall in
Chicago. His uncanny instinct for exciting programs invariably
received rave reviews. Once he explained how he selected his
photographic subjects:

> If I am walking through Brussels and see a dog cart or some
> other unimportant thing that is interesting enough for me to
> watch it, I am totally certain others would be interested in seeing
> a photograph of it.

A conservative man, Holmes avoided political upheavals,
economic exploitation, and social conflicts in his travelogues.
"When you discuss politics," he said, "you are sure to offend."
Holmes focused on people, places, and customs. He offered his
audience a world which was unfailingly tranquil and beautiful.

In 1897, Holmes introduced motion picture segments into his
programs. ("Neapolitans Eating Spaghetti" was his first film
clip.) His engaging personality contributed to his success. His

crisp narrative was delivered in a pleasant and cultured tone. He always wore formal dress with striped pants before an audience. Holmes took pride in creating an atmosphere so that his listeners could imagine the "Magic of Mexico" or the "Frivolities of Paris." "My first ambition was to be a magician," he said. "And, I never departed from creating illusions. I have tried to create the illusion that we are going on a journey. By projecting the views, I tried to create the illusion we are looking through 'the window of travel' upon shifting scenes." Holmes's travelogues were immensely successful financially—and Holmes became one of history's most indefatigable travelers.

Holmes's lectures took place during the winter months between the 1890s and his retirement in the early 1950s. In between, he traveled—he crossed Morocco on horseback from oasis to oasis (1894); he was in the Philippines during the 1899 insurrection; in 1901, he traversed the Russian Empire, going from Moscow to Vladivostok in 43 days. He visited Yellowstone National Park (1896) before it had been fully mapped. He was always on the move, traveling to: Venice (1896); London (1897); Hawaii (1898); The Philippines (1899); Paris (1900); Russia, China, and Korea (1901-02); Madeira, Lisbon, Denmark, and Sweden (1902); Arizona, California, and Alaska (1903); Switzerland (1904); Russia and Japan (1905); Italy, Greece, Egypt, and Hong Kong (1906); Paris, Vienna, and Germany (1907); Japan (1908); Norway (1909); Germany and Austria (1910); Brazil, Argentina, and Peru (1911); Havana and Panama (1912); India and Burma (1913); the British Isles (1914); San Francisco (1915); Canada (1916); Australia and New Zealand (1917); Belgium and Germany (1919); Turkey and the Near East (1920); England (1921); China (1922); North Africa (1923); Italy (1924); Ceylon (1925); Holland (1926); France (1927); Spain (1928); London (1929); Ethiopia (1930); California (1931); Java (1932); Chicago (1933); the Soviet Union (1934); Normandy and Brittany (1935); South America (1936); South Africa (1937); Germany (1938).

Holmes's black and white photographs have extraordinary clarity. His sharp eye for the unusual ranks him as a truly outstanding photographer and chronicler of the world.

Holmes's lectures on the Panama Canal were his most popular—cities added extra sessions. For Holmes though, his favorite presentation was always Paris—"no city charms and fascinates us like the city by the Seine." He found Athens in the morning to be the most beautiful scene in the world—"with its pearl lights and purple-blue shadows and the Acropolis rising in mystic grandeur." Above all though, Japan remained his favorite land— "one can peel away layer after layer of the serene contentment which we mistake for expressionlessness and find new beauties and surprises beneath each." And Kyoto, once the capital, was the place he wanted most to revisit—and revisit. Holmes never completed a travelogue of New York City—"I am saving the biggest thing in the world for the last." At the time of his death in 1958 at age 88, Holmes had visited most of the world. He repeatedly told interviewers that he had lived an exciting and fulfilling life because he had accomplished his goal—to travel.

In a time before television, Burton Holmes was for many people "The Travelogue Man." He brought the glamour and excitement of foreign lands to Americans unable to go themselves. His successful career spanned the years from the Spanish-American War in 1898 to the Cold War of the 1950s—a period when Americans were increasingly curious about distant places and peoples. During this time period, travel was confined to a comparative handful of the privileged. Holmes published travelogues explaining foreign cultures and customs to the masses.

In this series of splendid travel accounts, Holmes unfolds before our eyes the beauties of foreign lands as they appeared almost a century ago. These volumes contain hundreds of photographs taken by Holmes. Through his narratives and illustrations we are transported in spirit to the most interesting countries and cities of the world.

BERLIN

The cities of Hamburg and Berlin that Burton Holmes describes in this 1907 travelogue no longer exist. World War II (1939-45) destroyed them. Therefore, Holmes's text and photographs are of historical importance. The buildings, street scenes, and people in folk dress that he photographed have disappeared.

The Proclamation of the German Empire on January 18, 1871, was an outstanding event in 19th-century history. The unification of Germany added another great power to the family of European nations, and Berlin became the capital. The effect was a population boom of unforeseen proportion. In 1871, the city had approximately 825,000 inhabitants; in 1907, the year of Holmes's visit, the population had reached almost three million. Tenements were constructed almost overnight to house the new labor force that was employed to transform Berlin into a grand imperial capital. Property speculation reached a fever pitch, allowing many Berliners to make quick fortunes. This mass housing boom established Berlin's reputation for having the largest concentration of tenements in the world.

Kaiser William II (1888-1918) strove to make Berlin a city worthy of a mighty empire. Massive public buildings were constructed. The rural road called Kurfurstendamm was transformed into a splendid boulevard, and Berlin became a magnet for artists and scientists. It also attracted increasing numbers of the unemployed, as William II transformed Germany into an industrial giant. Between 1882 and 1913, the number of factory workers rose from six million to thirteen million. Especially notable was the expansion of pig iron production and the output of coal, and even more phenomenal was the development of the electrical industry. Germany also held an undisputed supremacy in the manufacture of chemicals. In brief, by 1914, Germany had become a leading industrial power. Among European nations, it yielded precedence only to Great Britain in the gross value of its manufacturers.

During the same period, the German army and navy more than doubled in size. Army appropriations increased 350 percent and naval expenditures soared more than 600 percent.

This industrialization and militarism impressed Holmes, who thought Kaiser William II was preparing for war. "We see him in photographs or in person . . . reviewing troops on the Tempel-hoferfeld. We see him as an equestrian in the Tiergarten, as a pedestrian in Unter-den-Linden or as the helmeted war-lord in the imperial car, motoring like a hurricane from Mars across the Potsdamer Platz. Berlin without the Kaiser would seem to lack one-half of its population." Holmes perceptively notes the crushing taxes on the "plain people" to supply the army with powder and with steel. "Is this monstrous thing of blood and discipline—this German army—worth what it costs the people in gold, in labor, and in sacrifice?" he asks.

It is this pulsating imperial city of Berlin and the thriving port of Hamburg in 1907 that Holmes describes. He gives us a unique portrait of these two cities as they were transformed by William II.

Berlin

THE city that is without dignity or beauty can never be more than a camping-place for the workers of the world.

The map of the United States is dotted with industrial camps, crowded with busy and ambitious men and women. Some of these camps shelter populations numbering hundreds of thousands. They are marvelous centers of all that is most marvelous in modern life. To such great camps we give the name of cities, but we do not give them that which should be the crowning glories of a city, order and cleanliness and beauty. Most of them are centers of unsightliness, surrounded by areas of costly ugliness and splendid squalor. Some of us are conscious of the lack of those things that make for beauty, quietude, and comfort in our cities; others are quite content with conditions as they are. To such I can say nothing, save to congratulate them on their lack of sensitiveness

"AUF WIEDERSEHEN"

to unpleasant sights and jarring sounds. They doubtless would applaud the proud and prosperous citizen of a wealthy western metropolis who voiced their sentiments when he said, in answer to some fastidious criticism of the ugliness that is to-day characteristic of American cities, "What's the use of beauty? We're out for the stuff." To this, hundreds of old-world cities will reply that beauty *pays:* witness the millions annually spent by beauty-hungry Americans in those European cities, great and small, which have made themselves agreeable to the eye and pleasing to the senses of those who seek respite from the banality and turmoil of our urban existence. Nearly every one of those foreign cities has its lesson for us; especially valuable is the lesson of Berlin. The lesson begins at the pier in Hoboken, New Jersey — a town that is the "Gate to Germany" for the majority of American travelers. German neatness and trimness, German thoroughness and discipline, have nearly succeeded in passing the United States Customs at Hoboken; we find them in all the fullness of their orderly dignity on board the gigantic German ships that lie between the splendid new steel piers of the German Lloyd and the

FACING A GALE

LEAVING HOBOKEN

A FLOATING HOTEL

Hamburg-American Line. From the deck of one of those magnificent floating hotels, as it glides down the North River, we watch the amazing panorama of New York — that astounding succession of sky-scrapers that do not astound us, simply because we ourselves have seen them increase in height and multiply in number from year to year; we shall see nothing more astounding in the Old World, rest assured of that. But two hours later this most wonderful, if not most beautiful, of cities has sunk below the far horizon in the west, and we watch the sun sink to rest behind the fog banks that obscure the shores of the land we leave behind — the land we love — the great land, richer in possibilities, and, considering its brief life as a nation, richer in achievement than any of the lands toward which we go. To them we go, not to ask the secrets of success, not to find the source of energy and

enterprise — these we have already
found. We go abroad to ask how
we may best enjoy the success that
has already crowned our efforts,
how we may best use the fruits of
that vaster success that is sure to
crown our future enterprise. We
go abroad, not to acquire a disdain
for the life and the ideals of our
own land, but to acquire knowledge of the life and the ideals of
an older world, a world which
naturally is in some ways wiser,
a world which has been enjoying

DER KUTSCHER

THE NEW CENTRAL STATION IN HAMBURG

leisure while we have been so feverishly busy building up our wonderful New World. The people over there have had time to think out and solve certain problems, which we have not yet had time to take up. Yet we cannot say that the Old World has been idle all this time. There is a distinction between being idle and enjoying a leisure earned by serious and thoughtful effort. Germany has not been idle these past forty years; the ship that carries us across the sea, one of the many ships belonging to the most important steamship company in all the world to-day — a German company — is evidence that Germany has not only been hard at work but has in fact done a thousand times better than the United States in developing her commerce on the seas. German ships carry a large share of the mails of England and the United States. German ships serve as

OVER THE ELBE

transports for the ever-increasing army of American tourists that annually invades England and the Continent. German industry now looms more threateningly than German militarism. The world now looks almost with awe upon the German laborer—the Teutonic builder, strong, patient, painstaking, and

A MODERN THOR

A TEUTONIC TOILER

content with little pay. The toiler of new Germany, as typified
by the splendid specimen of manhood in one of our illustrations,
looks a reincarnation of some Northern god. He looks a two-eyed
Wotan; he also realizes our ideal of Thor, the belted God of
Thunder, ready to fling his crushing hammer — that magic
hammer that returned to his strong hand each time that he as
the champion of the old Norse gods flung it amongst their enemies.

German industry has flung many a crushing hammer into
the factories of France and England; and the French and
the English working-men are still wondering what hit them. It
will be our turn next, unless we learn to be less wasteful and to

THE JUNGFERNSTIEG AND THE BINNEN-ALSTER

THE RATHAUS OF HAMBURG

live within our means. The growth of the German industries in the last quarter-century has been phenomenal; statistics tell a thoroughly amazing tale for which we cannot find space in our travelogue. Suffice it to say that since the Franco-Prussian War, United Germany has advanced from a real, all-pervading poverty to a prosperity that astonishes

TROLLEY DE LUXE

even the men who have guided the nation on its rapid and triumphant way. We feel prosperity in the very atmosphere as we walk the streets of Hamburg, now the greatest seaport of the Continent. Although the population numbers less than nine hundred thousand, Hamburg is rivaled in the volume of her tonnage only by New York, Liverpool, and London, ranking with them as one of the four most important commercial cities in the Occidental world — for we must not forget the great Oriental port, Hongkong. It is a busy city, as devoted to its business as any city of our own, and yet Hamburg does not disdain beauty. The citizens of Hamburg have not been too busy to beautify their city, not too engrossed with their commercial interests to keep their streets clean and their skies free from smoke. They have even gone in for artistic trolley cars, with

NOT A SKY-SCRAPER, MERELY A SCAFFOLDING

windows as big as those of a club and glazed with genuine plate glass and draped with rich green curtains that harmonize with the pale canary color of the car. The fare is ten pfennigs — two and one-half cents. The motorman and the conductor are in uniform. They wear caps like those of the German soldiers, and they salute us with automatic courtesy before asking for our fare. This makes us feel that we are far from home — until we catch sight of what we think to be the skeleton of a skyscraper in construction. I should

ON THE AUSSEN-ALSTER

say cloud-scratcher, for *Wolkenkratzer* — cloud-scratcher — is the name applied by the Germans to American steel structures. But the Hamburg structure that has caught our eye is not made of steel; it is not a prospective *Wolkenkratzer*. It is not even a building; it is merely the wooden scaffolding, inside of which a seven-story house of solid stone is about to be erected. When

THE LOMBARDS-BRÜCKE

the house is finished the cage of scaffolding inside of which it has developed will be removed.

Two little rivers flow through Hamburg. They look more like canals, but before discharging into the greater river Elbe they widen out, forming two large placid basins of fresh water in the very heart of the town. The smaller of these two pretty lakes, the Binnen-Alster, is one mile in circumference, and is overlooked by Hamburg's best hotels and the tall towers of the many churches. Small steamers ply like water-omnibuses from port to port, bringing the business men to town, or taking them, late in the afternoon, back to their pretty homes in that park-like residential region on the shores of the still larger outer basin, called the Aussen-Alster, which is the aquatic playground of the city. The early evening sees it alive with sailing craft. Numerous rowing clubs practice on its smooth surface every day, and on Sundays informal regattas are participated in by all sorts of craft, sailed, rowed, or steered by the sons of the men who own the big, real ships that make the name of Hamburg known and respected on the ocean highways of the commercial world. There is method in the

THE HAMBURG OF TO-DAY

THE HAMBURG OF YESTERDAY

madness of these pleasure-seekers on the Aussen-Alster; they
know that their city's hold on wealth and power lies with the hand
that sets the sail and grips the wheel.
They are the men who to-mor-
row will take up the complex
duties of directing the
movements of the mer-
chant fleets that throng
the anchorage and line
the docks of Hamburg's

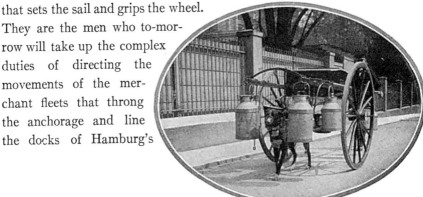

A DOG'S LIFE

port, the most modern and best equipped great seaport in the world. It is well worth our while to make a short cruise through that port amid the forest of masts and funnels rising above the busy waters cf the Elbe, the river that carries Ham-burg's commerce to the sea.

This harbor of Hamburg, five miles in length, affords accommo-dation for seven thousand boats, from the flat river-barges to the eight-deck trans-Atlantic liners. The greater part of it is a free harbor or bonded warehouse enclos-ure covering twenty-five hund-red acres of both land and water. The imports for a recent year represented about four thousand mil-lion marks, about a billion dollars, and the exports represented only a trifle less.

Hamburg has been modernized through her misfor-tunes. Plundered and wrecked by Napoleon's soldiers under Davoût in

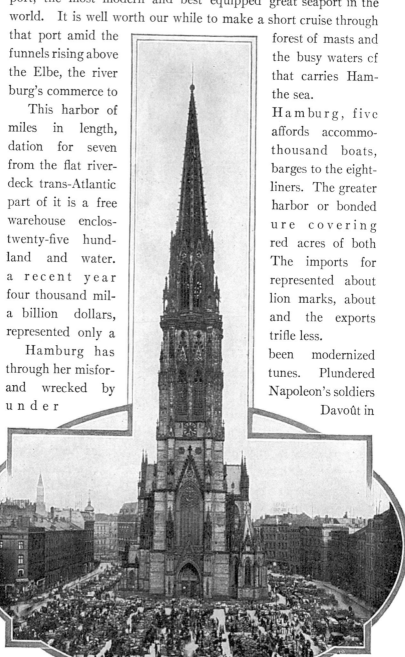

THE CHURCH OF ST. NICHOLAS

1813, laid low by fire in 1842, and ravaged by the cholera in 1892, this great free city — once one of the queens of the Hanseatic League, the largest of the three great Hanse towns of Germany — has repaired the ravages of war, risen in modern splendor from the ashes of conflagrations, and, warned by pestilence, taught herself the costly lesson of modern sanitation. Hamburg is now one of the richest, best built, and healthiest of seaports. The city of Hamburg, with about a hundred and fifty square miles of the region roundabout, forms a little republic, joined by her own consent to the German Empire but governing herself through her own Burgerschaft and Senate. The little state, however, sends three representatives to the Reichstag and one to the Bundesrat of Imperial Germany. The

IN THE HOPFEN MARKET

ENTRANCE TO HAGENBECK'S ZOÖLOGICAL PARK

sights of Hamburg are sights that are easy to see, sights that do not tire the

OUT OF THE EAST

THE TEACHER OF MERCY

tourist. To see the most conspicuous, he has but to look up at Hamburg's spires, the tallest of them the spire of the Church of St. Nicholas, ranking as the fourth highest in all Europe — its cross four hundred and eighty-five feet above the pavement of the crowded Hopfen-Markt.

Then to see the most curious of Hamburg's sights let the tourist take a trolley out to the ideal "Zoo," recently created by the master-mind of Carl Hagenbeck. No city in the world possesses so

HAGENBECK'S WONDERLAND

wonderful an exhibition of wild animals and nowhere in the world save in the wildernesses and the jungles or on the mountain-slopes or the ice-floes, can we see the splendid savage creatures of the animal kingdom so thoroughly at home, so completely in the picture. In Hagen-beck's wonderland each creature finds itself placed in it's prop-er habitat. The lions have their lairs in the rocky ravines, the cham-

FROM THE FAR SOUTH

ois have their abrupt mountain-walls on which to practice dizzy feats of animal alpinism, the pen-guins and the polar bears have their white antarctic world, — that at least looks as cold as the South Pole,—and the elephants, as they pass, guided by Ceylonese mahouts, recognize the images of the Buddha worshipped in the land from which they come. Thus all creation feels at home at Hagenbeck's, and there all created things appear to dwell together in peace in absolute freedom — apparent

IN THE HARBOR OF HAMBURG

freedom only —
for while no bar-
riers or cages are
conspicuous, there
do exist deep de-
pressions and
moats, dissembled
hedges and fences,
that prevent any
tragic mingling of
the lion and the
lamb or the man-
eater and the man.

A MODERN PIER

But of all the sights of Hamburg the most impressive is the new monument of Prince Bismarck. It is more impressive even than the great harbor with its teeming fleets that tell of Germany's far-reaching enterprise, for in this Bismarck monument the progress and power of the whole nation seem to stand personified.

Wherever the traveler may go in Germany, the face and form of Bismarck, cast in bronze or chiseled in stone or marble, will rise before him; but this Bis-marck *Denkmal* in Hamburg — the latest and greatest of the many hundreds of monuments that have been raised in honor of the Iron Chancellor— towers above all the others

BISMARCK

in artistic worth and in a certain indescribable impressiveness.
It looms above us like power personified. I
must repeat the phrase — I cannot otherwise
express that sense of power, of determina-
tion, of inevitableness, that overwhelms
us as we look up at this grim colossus,
this stone glorification of the greatest

THE NEW BISMARCK DENKMAL IN HAMBURG

IN THE KIEL CANAL

of great Germans. No other statesman has a more secure hold upon the gratitude and the respect of a great nation. Ask any German wheresoever you may find him, "Who is the greatest man your nation has produced?" and nine out of ten will answer with enthusiasm "Bismarck." But Germany did not produce Bismarck, *he produced Germany.* He was the J. P. Morgan of world-politics. He formed the greatest political trust of modern times. He organized the German

THE KAISER AT SEA

WILLIAM II

Empire. He was more than a king-maker. He made kaisers of kings; kingdoms and principalities and petty states he welded into a world-power of imperial proportions.

The German Empire is the newest of the great powers; its capital, Berlin, is the most modern of all the greater Continental cities. Although Berlin became the residence of the Hohenzollern family five centuries ago, it was not until the time of Frederick the Great that it became a place of real importance. Even at the end of his long reign—that is to say at the time of our Revolution,—Berlin had a population of less than a hundred and fifty thousand. To-day there are nearly three million people living in Berlin. Of these one man stands out as the most conspicuous, pervading personality of living Germany—the Kaiser.

William the Second is everywhere, interested in all things, active in all things, *himself* in all things. He has an insatiable appetite for information: as a giver of advice he is indefatigable. We see him in pictures or in person questioning his admirals on

THE KAISER AT MANŒUVERS

the bridges of his war-ships, directing his staff officers at military manœuvers or reviewing troops on the Tempelhoferfeld. We see him as an equestrian in the Tiergarten, as a pedestrian in Unter-den-Linden or as the helmeted war-lord in the imperial car, motoring like a hurricane from Mars across the

THE KAISER AND HIS SONS

Potsdamer Platz. Berlin without the Kaiser would seem to
lack one-half of its three million population.

The business center of the Kaiser's capital may be said to lie
near the intersection of the Friedrich Strasse and the Leipziger

FRIEDRICH STRASSE AND LEIPZIGER STRASSE

Strasse, two of Berlin's most animated thoroughfares, but the focal
point of Berlin life is where the Friedrich Strasse crosses the
broader, finer, and more famous avenue called Unter-den-Linden.
There the streams of pleasure and business meet and mingle.
The Friedrich Strasse is a narrow, crowded canal of commerce:
Unter-den-Linden is a broad, calm river of luxury and leisure.
It is the nearest approach in Berlin to a Parisian Boulevard.
Our picture of this famous urban cross-roads is taken from the
balcony of the almost equally famous Café Bauer, taken in spite

of the protests of the waiter and without the consent of the pro-
prietor, for on asking his permission to make pictures from the
balcony on which we sat as patrons of his establishment, the crafty
but short-sighted individual refused, saying that pictures taken
from his balcony always showed and advertised, not so much his

FRIEDRICH STRASSE AND UNTER-DEN-LINDEN

own establishment, the Café Bauer, but rather the rival establishment, the Victoria Café across the way! To temper our disap-
pointment — not realizing that while he "*verboted*" we were taking
both the *verboten* snap-shots and the *verboten* motion pictures — he
assured us that the outlook from the Victoria was much more
effective, including as it did the façade of the Café Bauer. Just
to spite our ungracious host, I refrain from publishing a picture
of his celebrated café — which, however, will not thereby suffer

POTSDAMER PLATZ

AN ADVERTISING COLUMN

loss of custom, for no stranger can miss it — even though it fail to figure pictorially in our travelogue.

At first glance the shopping streets of Berlin might be mistaken for streets in an American city. The buildings, the shop-fronts, and show-windows offer little that is unfamiliar; and the shoppers, though not so smart in appearance as those of Fifth Avenue, would pass as New Yorkers, one

block east or west, on Fourth or Sixth. The tide of traffic rushes with as great speed but with less noise than that of our cities. The motor-bus and taxicab are much in evidence — but the horse-drawn bus with its low body and small wheels still zigzags along like an old-style horse-car off the rails. On Sundays the Berlin merchant not only shuts up shop, but even covers up his shop. Elaborate canvas curtains, sometimes artistically decorated, are stretched before the big plate-glass show-windows — on the outside of the pane; smaller curtains cover the little show-cases that are placed between the windows — and the fine mirrors that face the sidewalk and on week days afford the ladies so many opportunities to make sure that their hats are on straight are, on Sundays, swathed also in their Sabbath shrouds. The policing

PERIODICALS AND DAILIES

SUNDAY IN THE SHOPPING DISTRICT

of Berlin is perfect.   At every important corner are two personifi-
cations of law and order, one mounted, one on foot.   They appear
to do nothing but *be there* — that is quite enough to insure obedi-

SABBATH SWATHING

ence to the well-
understood traffic
regulations and re-
spect for law and
order.   One day,
however, I wit-
nessed an arrest:
two men quarrel-
ing had proceeded
from verbal insults
to bloody blows.
Both were livid
with rage, but
when the *Schutz-*

SCHUTZMANN

mann approached they broke away and stood quietly by while he questioned the onlookers. Satisfied that the fault was all on one side, the policeman tapped the aggressor on the shoulder, called a taxicab, politely invited his prisoner to step in; the prisoner, without a word of protest, accepts the invitation, the taxi rolls away, and the crowd quietly disperses. The influ-  ence of the uniform is irresistible. The brass button hypnotizes the plain people. The word "*verboten*" is a fetish worshiped by the commoner. A clever Frenchman has said that the Prussian lives in discipline like a fish in water.

According to the same Gallic critic, Berlin is "a city of contrasts: American, yet helmeted with steel; an ultra-modern setting, where tradition remains all powerful." Yet he feels the presence of an unseen something, fine and beautiful, and calls Berlin "The City of the Inner Dream."

"Music," he says, "pleads for Berlin." In the eyes of the American, it is cleanliness that pleads most eloquently for Berlin. The art of municipal housekeeping is practiced there in perfection. Berlin is the best kempt great city in the world. Berlin is practically slumless. There are rich quarters, other quarters not so rich, but no quarter that declares itself in outward aspect

THE WERTHEIMER WARENHAUS

as a poor quarter, absolutely no quarter that advertises its misery. Poverty and misery may exist in Berlin, but it is a self-respecting poverty, a decent misery that brushes its clothes and combs its hair, just as conscientiously as the city itself polishes its house-fronts and washes its pavements. Municipal regard for the decencies of life breeds tidy homes and a tidy population, or is it that the virtues of a people naturally prone to neatness are reflected in the well-ordered aspect of their capital? At any rate, Berlin is an example and a model among cities. I have gone so far as to suggest from the platform that it would be a wise outlay of the public funds for any city in America to pay the expenses of its Mayor and Board of Aldermen for a little sight-seeing journey to Berlin and back. One of my kindly critics in reviewing the lecture asked, "Why back?" so I do not insist upon the return of the official tourists unless they have taken honestly to heart the splendid object-lesson offered by Berlin.

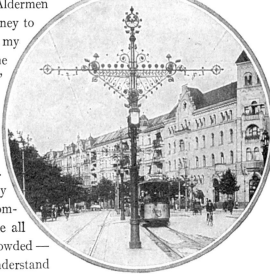

As for the Berlin trolley cars, they are clean and comfortable and cheap, but like all trolley cars, likely to be crowded — but not crowded as we understand the word. A Berlin car is full when

THE ARTISTIC TROLLEY POLES

all the seats are occupied, and the legally authorized number of passengers — usually five or six — have taken the *Stehplätze*, or "standing places," on the platform. Thus the German trolley

THE GRASSY TROLLEY TRACKS

car has its limitations: the American trolley car is never full. There is always room for a dozen more than the car can hold. We note also that the poles that support the electric wires need not be eyesores, that decorative standards will hold the wires just as well. We note also that all the rails are grooved rails, some are laid on special rights of way, paved, not with echoing

BUSINESS STREETS LIKE BOULEVARDS

granite blocks, but with green grass as nicely groomed as the green grass of our parks. 'T is no disparagement of Berlin to say that grass grows in her streets. Flowers and vines grow, too, in the *parterres* of the fine wide avenues along which we make our way through the newer part of town in the direction of Charlotten-burg. Old Berlin was not laid out on this grandly spacious plan: but the old crowded section of the city represents but a small portion of the metropolis of to-day. The vaster part of Berlin is brand-new, and in the making of it the people have profited by

A DEPARTMENT STORE

all the lessons of the past. Space, light, and air, easy communication, convenience, and beauty, have been regarded as more important than the question of mere cost. "What is it worth?" the German asks rather than "What will it cost?" Boundless as the long perspectives of these park-like city thoroughfares is our admiration for this

MODERN BERLIN

new Berlin of to-day as we go by tram or motor car, in taxicab or
auto-bus, along mile after mile of superb avenues, most of them
paved with asphalt, all with good pavements, smooth and clean,
all tram-car tracks with rails so carefully laid that crossing
them produces no jar; nor do the cars that run along those
rails jar on the ear like passing boiler factories on wheels. As

THERE IS AN ELEVATED RAILWAY IN THIS STREET!

for the elevated railway — the *Hochbahn* — of Berlin, it is almost invisible as well as practically inaudible. For example, look
along the Bülow Strasse — in our illustration. There is an
elevated railway in this street. There *is*. You cannot see it;
you can scarcely hear the trains as they slip by, behind that screen
of foliage; but the "L" is there, and if you will step to the left,
between those rows of trees that border the central promenade of
the Bülow Strasse, you will find yourself in a long cloister of which
the columns are the steel supports of the elevated structure,
which forms a sheltering roof. Above run the almost silent
electric trains, below the calm and pensive citizen may sit or stroll

THE ALLÉE UNDER THE "L"

in shady comfort on hot days, or dry-shod when the weather is wet. And there beneath that Berlin "L" I sat a while and strolled a while and mused about the corner of Van Buren Street and Wabash Avenue, Chicago. Have you ever stood at that noisy corner at the awful hour of the homeward rush, waiting for *your* car, while "L" trains thundered and crashed around the curves above, and trolley cars thundered and crashed along the rails below, and drays and wagons thundered and clattered by, and automobiles zigzaged and skidded over the rough stones, sounding their siren horns? If so, you doubtless will agree with me in holding that at that infernal corner there is one "L" above and another "L" below. But

THE "L" CONCEALED BY TREES

A SUBWAY ENTRANCE

waking from this retrospective nightmare I wandered on beneath that Berlin elevated line until I reached the Nollendorf Platz. I looked up at the picturesque "L" station and at first mistook it for an elevated Palm House or Horticultural Hall. It is a curious but graceful structure, light and airy and inviting; it adorns rather than mars the pretty square; it proves that the practical need not of necessity be hideous, as it usually

"L" STATION IN THE NOLLENDORF PLATZ

is with us. There is no express service, the line being a simple double track; the speed is not astonishing, but what is astonishing, at least to an American, is the fact that *the passengers themselves* are allowed to open and to close the doors of the cars as the train arrives at or leaves the station. Imagine leaving the doorman's strenuous duties to the passengers in the subway

THE ORIENTAL GATE OF THE " ZOO "

or on the elevated in New York! Such a course would kill off half the population the first month. Nothing makes us feel farther away from home than to see the placid Berliners letting themselves calmly in and out of their *Hochbahn* trains, and living to repeat the operation day after day. We let ourselves out at the Zoölogical Garden, which is one of the most popular resorts in Berlin—more like a concert garden or an out-of-door café than like a mere menagerie. All Berlin throngs the paths of the " Zoo " on pleasant afternoons and evenings: bands are playing, beer is flowing, flirtations—if we may so far stretch the meaning

of the word — are proceeding, and all
creation, including the wild animals.
appears happy and content.
We, as students of styles rather
than species, find the fauna
less interesting than the flora
on view in the garden, and
by flora I mean the artificial
flora, the millinery on the
heads of Berlin belles.

Berlin cannot be
called a stylish city; that
is, what we are pleased
to call style is rarely seen.
There is no German " Gib-
son Girl" and no Teutonic
"Fluffy Ruffles." There are

"THERE IS NO GERMAN GIBSON GIRL"

no amazing creatures robed like birds of paradise such as we
see in Paris, and even the lady of the trim-cut tailor-made is
conspicuously absent. Instead, we see fine,
wholesome types of womanhood, who
waste no time on niceties of dress;
they are content merely to be well
clad. Their clothes are not *cre-
ations*, they are merely clothes;
their hats are not "dreams" as
in Paris, not "nightmares" as
ofttimes in New York, — they
are simply hats. The Marcel
wave will never swamp Berlin.

The most artistically dressed
women that we saw in Berlin
were the nurse-maids, those
wholesome, sturdy girls who wear

" . . . NO TEUTONIC FLUFFY RUFFLES!"

the curious old Wendish costume of their country district, a district that we are to visit later on. It is called the Spreewald; its daughters, who come up to town by scores for domestic service in the city, are called *Spreewälderinnen.*

If you see a girl with a picturesque cap, like a huge flaring bow, on her head and a baby-carriage in front of her, you may be sure she is one of those *Spreewälderinnen.*

THE SPREEWALD NURSES IN BERLIN

They are never seen without the *Tücher*, and rarely without the perambulator. Scores of them are to be seen daily in Berlin's great park, the beautiful

A PROMENADE

Tiergarten, whither they come from the adjacent aristocratic quarters with the babies of Berlin's first families snugly bestowed in an artistic *Kinderwagen*. With them come also older *Kinder* to play in the nearest sandy *Spielplatz*, provided by a paternal administration for the joy and benefit of the lively little Prussians who there work off a lot of surplus energy, building sand forts or digging little Kiel Canals. The games of little Germans seem naturally to take a military turn, and when we tried to photograph them at their play, they at first insisted on falling in and standing stiffly and grimly at salute before the camera. It cost some little diplomacy to induce them to drop their military poses and "look pleasant."

IN THE TIERGARTEN

The Tiergarten is a park almost exactly the size of Hyde Park in London—about six hundred acres—nearly as large as Central Park, New York. Until the eighteenth century it was, as the name implies, an "animal garden," a deer park, where the Grand Electors and the Kings of Prussia held their hunting parties. To-day the wild game has all disappeared, but you could not fire a gun in the Tiergarten without hitting a marble statue.

LITTLE "SPIELERS"

The woods are full of them. At night we see them gleaming in the

IN A "SPIELPLATZ"

wood like listening ghosts, whiter than the moonbeams that fall
upon them. On either side of the long Sieges Allée, or Avenue
of Victory, rise the marble effigies of Prussia's rulers, thirty-two
of them, each on a pedestal, behind each one a marble hemicycle,
set against a background of deep green. All this magnificent
array of marble royalty is the gift of William II, paid for by the
Kaiser from his private purse. He honors thus his predecessors
and ancestors from the first Margrave, Albert the Bear, who ruled
the little Mark of Brandenburg about seven hundred and fifty
years ago, down to William I, who bequeathed to his successors
the new-formed empire, which under William II has become a
great world-power. We may read the history of Prussia's rise in
the faces of her rulers as we pass them in review. In the fifth
hemicycle from that of Albert are the Margraves, John and Otho,
who ruled jointly during the middle years of the thirteenth century;
behind them busts of the Magistrate Marsilius and Simeon, the

THE SIEGES ALLÉR

THE MARGRAVES, JOHN AND OTHO

Provost of Berlin, two of the great men of that double reign. Directly opposite stands the hemicycle of Frederick the Great, the Prussian King whose reign stands in the fifth place from the modern end of this long line of rulers. Behind the almost puny form of Frederick the Great are busts of two great contemporaries of that brilliant monarch,—one is Sebastian Bach, father of modern music, the other is Schwerin, field-marshal of Frederick in his victorious campaigns. After Frederick the Great there were only four Prussian Kings; the last one, William the Great, became the first Emperor of the new German Empire. His monument is so placed that the first German Kaiser faces the first medieval Margrave of little Brandenburg, while stretching away down the great Sieges Allée are thirty more white statues of the thirty Margraves, Electors, and Kings whose reigns intervened between those of Albert the Bear, who died in 1170, and William the Great, who died in 1888. A striking vista of this grandiose memorial avenue may be enjoyed from the top of the Sieges Säule. This "Victory Column" is two hundred feet in height, built of dark stone and granite and encircled by three rings of captured cannon,

RULERS OF PRUSSIA

most of which were taken from the French. Above, a gilded figure, forty-eight feet high, representing Borussia, or Prussia, upholds a laurel wreath, as if about to crown the victorious German monarchs and their great military leaders, whose statues are ranged along the Sieges Allée or in the circular platz below —around the Sieges Säule. This Königs Platz is no pleasant place for Frenchmen. Everything here recalls the bitter days of 1870 and 1871. In one direction the long line of more or less petty monarchs of the once small, poor Prussian state. In another direction the rich Reichstags-Gebäude, the Imperial Diet of the mighty modern empire, a building paid for with a part of the enormous war indemnity — five billions of francs — ex-   acted by a

FREDERICK THE GREAT

victorious Germany from a crushed and bleeding France. The structure cost about five and a half million dollars. The interior is superbly decorated. The most important feature is the Hall of the Diet, where sit the three hundred and

WILLIAM THE GREAT

THE AVENUE OF VICTORY

ninety-seven members of the Reichstag. There is a small hall used by the fifty members of the Bundesrat or Federal Council when they assemble during the sessions of the larger body: at other times the Council meets at the Imperial Home Office in the Wilhelm Strasse. In one of the corridors we see, spelled out in gilded letters, each letter supported by a sculptured figure, a motto that should have a place in the legislative palaces of every land — "Erst das Vaterland, dann die Partie," "First the Fatherland, then the Party." Perhaps the most significant thing that strikes the thoughtful observer is the fact that it is here in this costly and magnificent hall of the imperial parliament that the socialists — call them Social Democrats if you prefer — have made their party a *recognized* party, a party that plays an important rôle in the politics of the nation.

It is an amazing fact that the German Empire, theoretically an autocracy, should be one of the most advanced nations in the world along lines of what would have been called a few years ago "socialistic legislation"; witness the old age pension system, and the laws establishing compuls- ory insurance of labor- ers in case of accident, sickness, disability, or superannuation. Yet all these laws which enable the Empire to stand as the only beg- garless great nation in the world were initia- ted, not by the new and powerful labor party, but by the old Emperor William I, who in his message to the Reichstag in No- vember, 1881, said: "Those who are dis- abled in consequence of old age or infirmity possess a well-founded claim to a more ample relief on the part of the State than they have hitherto enjoyed. To devise the fittest ways and means for

THE COLUMN OF VICTORY

making such provisions, however difficult, is one of the highest
obligations of every community based on the moral foundations of
Christianity.   A more intimate connection with the actual capabili-
ties of the people and a mode of turning these to account in corpo-
rate associations will, under the patronage and with the aid of the

THE REICHSTAG

State, we trust, develop a scheme to solve which the State alone
would prove unequal."

The invalid and old age pension law was put in practice in
1891.   Premiums for accident insurance are paid entirely by the
employer.   In case of disability the man receives two thirds of
his regular wages; in case of death the family receives fifteen per
cent of his annual pay in a lump sum, and annual payments equal-
ing sixty per cent of his earning capacity when he died.   Premiums
for insurance against sickness are paid, one third by the employer,
two thirds by the employee.   In case of sickness the man receives
half pay and medical attendance.   Insurance against old age is

obligatory for all wage-workers who are over the age of sixteen
and earning less than five hundred dollars a year. Contributions
corresponding to premium payments and ranging from three to
nine cents are turned in weekly by the workers in the form of
stamps, like postage stamps, which they purchase at a local office

BISMARCK

or which are purchased for them and charged against their wages
by the employer. The pensions, granted to all who pass the age of
seventy-one years, range from about thirty to sixty dollars a year,
including the imperial subsidy of about twelve dollars, the gift of
the Empire. It would require too much space to go further into
detail. It is enough to say that this seemingly Utopian scheme is
working out successfully. Enormous sums are paid out daily,
enormous sums lie in reserve, employers make their profit, and
Germany has no pauper problem.

In front of the Reichstags-Gebäude stands a bronze figure
of the Imperial Chancellor, of heroic proportions, a Bismarck

twenty feet tall, with one hand gripping a sword, the other resting upon the charter of the foundation of the Empire. Below, around the pedestal, are placed other colossal figures. In front, Atlas with the weight of the world upon him; behind, Siegfried forging the Sword of Empire; on the right an heroic female figure— a personification of Constitutional Power crushing Revolt in the shape of a huge panther; to the left another imposing woman in bronze resting upon

ROON

a sphinx and gazing at a bronze document: this last composition may be intended to suggest the secret knowledge, the unspoken wisdom, that lay behind the statecraft of the great warrior-statesman on the pedestal above. But resuming our survey of the war-time reminders in the Königs Platz we glance at the commanding figure of Field-Marshal

VON MOLTKE

Count Roon, who was War Minister in 1870. Then on the western side of the Königs Platz, facing the bronze Bismarck, the man of blood and iron, we see the cold, calm, marble form of Von Moltke, the apparently bloodless, silent doer of the deeds that gave life and reality to the great aspirations and the imperious demands of his bigger but not greater partner in the affairs of '70 and '71. It may almost be said that the German Empire was made by these two men, Bismarck and Von Moltke; yet they toiled merely as faithful servants of their master, obedient subjects of their beloved king, William of Prussia, upon whose royal head they placed a new imperial crown. He sleeps, their king and emperor, the third man of that mighty trio, in the marble mausoleum at Charlottenburg not very far away. There in that Hall of Peace and Silence, in the golden glow that falls from amber windows, the Great Emperor, grandfather of the Kaiser of to-day, has slept since 1888; on his right hand lies his Empress Augusta. Beyond, side by side, repose the forms of Frederick William III and Queen Louise, his beautiful consort, the royal pair who reigned in Prussia during what the Germans call "the unfortunate

IN THE MAUSOLEUM AT CHARLOTTENBURG

war." Frederick William III saw his nation beaten by the French, his city and his palaces in the possession of Napoleon; but he saw also the downfall of the Man of Destiny, and his son, who now lies here in the same mausoleum, not only saw, but helped to precipitate the downfall of the third Napoleon, and amid the wreck of French ambitions saw the glory of a new Germany arise; he even saw himself proclaimed Emperor in the palace of the French Kings at Versailles. If dead kings hold converse in their tombs, what a satisfying tale could the son unfold to the father there in the mortuary temple at Charlottenburg.

ENTRANCE TO THE TOMB OF FREDERICK THE GREAT

Another royal sepulcher to which the traveler must make respectful pilgrimage is in the old Garrison Church of Potsdam, for there lies Frederick the Great. Even Napoleon himself paused in the tumult of a victorious campaign and like a tourist came to gaze upon the simple coffin of Prussia's most illustrious and most eccentric monarch — the king who first made Prussia great, the man

who was both the devoted friend and the jealous enemy of
the famous Frenchman, François Marie Arouet. The *nom de
plume* of that famous Frenchman is more familiar to us than his
rightful name, for François Marie Arouet was none other than
Voltaire. Frederick was a great admirer of the French; he loved

SANS SOUCI

their art, their mode of dress, and he professed to share their
philosophic views. Voltaire came to Potsdam as the guest of
Prussia's King, and for a time the two great little men enjoyed a
feast of reason and a flow of soul in the small plaything of a palace
called Sans Souci which was Frederick's favorite abode. But
the palace was not big enough to hold two such big egos at one
time. The King could not forget he was a king, and the Philosopher could not make his philosophy attain the end of all philosophy,
which is to put an end to strife and pain, to bring true peace on
earth, to cultivate good-will in the hearts of men. The monarch

who could brook the independent spirit of the
miller who refused to sell him the historic
Potsdam mill, which still stands proudly
at the royal gates, could not brook the
independent spirit of his great French
guest, and so Voltaire packed up his
books and papers and practically fled
from Sans Souci, where he had lived
for three years as the much loved and
admired friend of Prussia's autocrat.

Potsdam is to Berlin what Versailles was to Paris in the days when
there were kings in France; but where
the glory of Versailles lies in its palace,
its Trianons, and its artificial man-made

THE HISTORIC WINDMILL

gardens, Potsdam
owes more to Na-
ture than to man.
The site—an island
in the widespread
River Havel — is
one of great beau-
ty; the park of
Sans Souci and its
little bijou palace
are exquisite, but
the other palaces
are far from beau-
tiful and the build-
ings of the town
itself are of com-
monplace provin-

POTSDAM FROM THE RIVER

cial aspect save for the fine church of St. Nicholas, the dome of
which looms grandly above all the rest. Viewed from an ap-
proaching steamer, Potsdam looks like a great park or garden
dominated by that soaring dome; yet Potsdam is a city of more

THE CHURCH OF ST. NICHOLAS IN POTSDAM

than sixty thousand inhabitants with a garrison of seven thousand
troops. The city has been called "the cradle of the Prussian
army," and among the famous royal nurses who rocked that
cradle and tended the robust militant babe — that has now
become the biggest, strongest boy among the armies of the
world — were Frederick William I and his son, Frederick the
Great. The former always tried out his ideas of drill and discipline upon his pet corps, those gigantic Grenadiers of glorious
memory. Then he would summon to Potsdam the comparatively

HIGH ABOVE THE HAVEL

small officers and men of other regiments and himself instruct them how to become as good if not as big soldiers as their colossal models, the Royal Grenadiers. To this day the most perfect and picturesque military spectacle in Germany is the annual review of the garrison of Potsdam held in the Paradeplatz of the Town Palace within a few days of the greater but really less effective review of the Berlin garrison on the broad *Tempelhoferfeld*, which lies on the southern outskirts of the capital.

The traveler should not fail to prolong his river voyage up the Havel to the little town of Werder above which rise the famous hills which every year in April become the rendezvous of Berliners who love beauty —

AT WERDER

GEMÜTLICHES BEISAMMEN-SEIN!

and do not disdain beer. April is the season of the *Baumblüte*, the annual springtime flowering of the fruit trees on the slopes of Werder's hills. The spectacle is one that rivals the cherry-blossom festivals of old Japan; the massing of pale pinkish blossoms is magnificent, but we miss the picturesque details that make the Oriental

GARTEN KELLNER

flower fêtes so quaintly attractive. Instead of the dainty tea-
house garden of Japan, the crude beer garden common to all
Teutonic lands—instead of the smiling little *nesan* of that eastern
Fairyland, the scowling, bulky *Kellner* of this western Fatherland.
But there are always compensations; German beer is better than

A BERLIN MOTOR-BUS

the beer brewed in Japan, and the German crowds that sit and sip
that beer and gaze at the *Baumblüte* seem just as much in love
with Nature as the kimono-clad crowds that squat beneath the
cherry trees of Tokyo. In fact, the love of Nature is not monopo-
lized by any race; nor is the love of country. Every land is an
"Old Sod," a "Fatherland," a "Patrie," or a "God's Country"
in the eyes of those whose fathers came from it, whose hearts
remain in it. Apropos of that yearning for and pride in the land

from whence their fathers came, a letter — anonymous and if not honest at least amusing — that reached me a few years ago, before I had travelogued on any German subject, seems worth 're-reading here. It runs as follows, word for word just as traced by a methodical but apparently untrained hand upon three ragged sheets of very common paper:

Saint Louis, Mo., Feb. 15th '07.

Dear Mr. Holmes,

Me and my wife we have enjoyed your speeches and more yet your pictures of the old countrys. We have gon every time thar was lecturing and we hav even went to your Irish one some years back. You see my wife she is a irisher. Every time

A BERLIN TAXICAB

we think it is now about time for Mr. Holmes to come around wit his leckturs we look in the paper for the advertisemen of it and every time it makes me madder than ever because I do not see nothing in it about some pictures of the faderland (you see I am no irisher or no Norwayer) because she, my Mamie she tells our boy and our little girl well I gess there is nodding to see in germany else why dont he show 'some picturs of it. Dat makes me madder then more offit because I meinself was wonce on the Rhine and in Hamburg and Berlin and also in Kopniz so natural I know what is it in germany. We have a fine faderland.

So I write you if you have never been in germany, what?

SCHLAFEN SIE WOHL!

Lot of the people what go to your speeches is most germans or anyway they is germans by consent, and it would make them pleased if they can show ther boys and others what nice things there is where they was boys and girls together when they was yunger. Cant you show something onct of germany without mountains. Please Mr. Homes and oblige most respectfully one who was onct a german. A Friend.

The suburbs of Berlin are as admirably laid out as the city itself. Marvelous developments are now in progress and all the

A LAKE IN THE GRUNEWALD

beautiful forest region between the city and Potsdam will in time be transformed into a villa-city with perfect roadways traversing it in all directions, making all parts of the forest habitable and accessible without robbing it of its sylvan charm. The Germans must be descendants of the old forest tribes,—even the city-dwellers are tree lovers; all who can afford it have gardens with as many trees in them as possible; those who cannot afford a real garden devise a little imitation garden on a balcony or in one of the loggias so frequently found in the façades of the newer apartment buildings. But the ambition of every Berliner is to have a home in one of those green suburban forests, where he can enjoy not only his own trees but all the trees of his tree-loving neighbors.

This "return to the forest" was started by the men who founded what is called the Villa Colony of the Grunewald in 1889. It is

A GRUNEWALD VILLA

now one of the most attractive residential suburbs in the world, for with all the building of villas and laying out of streets and boulevards, they have kept always in view the preservation of the Grunewald itself, the ever "Green Wood" of coniferous trees. Thus hundreds, in fact thousands, of tired citizens of Berlin literally take to the woods after business hours: and on Sundays and holiday, thousands — nay, hundreds of thousands — of city-dwellers take to the taller timber of the farther reaches of the forest to spend their hours of leisure in the lap of Nature, breathing the perfume

A SPREEWALD COTTAGE

of the pines. But of all the holiday refuges for the people of Berlin there is one that is of unique charm, a rural region absolutely unlike any other in the world, easily accessible and at the same time, strange to say, practically unknown to the foreigner and rarely visited save by the Germans themselves, who know it well and love it well, but do not advertise its charm, lest it be invaded by the tourist army and ravaged by the regiments of globe-trotters that annually sweep over Germany, foraging for the picturesque and leaving in their wake the unwelcome aftermath of larger prices and heavier tips, smaller portions and lighter draughts of drinkables. This exquisite country district is called the Spree-wald — the "Forest of the Spree" — please pronounce it "Spray" for the Spree is a beautiful river, not a jamboree. It rises in Saxony, flows toward and through the city of Berlin, then joins the Havel which in turn joins the Elbe, which, as we have seen, passes through Hamburg and loses itself in the North Sea. The upper reaches of the River Spree, some sixty miles or more above Berlin, lie in a pretty *Wald* or wooded region, hence the name Spreewald. In this region dwells a small population differing in dress, in language, and in customs from the ordinary German population that surrounds this little Fatherland within a Fatherland. The dwellers in these pretty Spreewald cottages are not of Teutonic, they are of Slavic descent; they are generally called Wends or Wendish people. Another name for them is Sorbs or Sorbians. The encyclopedia tells us that they are natives of a country called Lusatia, and that Lusatia, after many political vicissitudes, after having belonged to Bohemia, and to Austria and even to Hungary, has at last been partitioned between Saxony and Prussia. The Spreewald is the last non-Germanized stronghold of the Wendish folk, who cling to all their old-time ways and

IN A WENDISH GARDEN

HOME, SWEET HOME

customs. Their cottages are quainter and more picturesque than those of their German neighbors, and their costumes, those of the women

at least, are without exception the quaintest and most picturesque that can be found in any part of Germany to-day. We have already noted the peculiar Wendish head-dress worn by the *Spreewälderinnen*, who serve as nurse-maids in Berlin. We find on reaching the Spreewald villages

THE TWO EXCEPTIONS

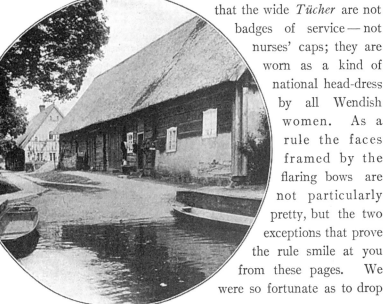

that the wide *Tücher* are not badges of service — not nurses' caps; they are worn as a kind of national head-dress by all Wendish women. As a rule the faces framed by the flaring bows are not particularly pretty, but the two exceptions that prove the rule smile at you from these pages. We were so fortunate as to drop

IN A WENDISH VENICE

in at the out-of-door studio of the village photographer just in time to see these two particularly charming damsels posing for their pictures. With their consent and that of our professional confrere we clicked our hand-cameras several times while he was getting ready to make a long time-exposure with his cumbrous old-style outfit. Possibly

ONE WENDISH SMILE

the dresses and the *Tücher* are a little more elaborate than would be worn every day; but the frank honest faces, the strong bare arms, and the happy dispositions pictured here are characteristic of the younger women in this forest region of the upper Spree: even the older women, the mothers of the Wendish tribe, seem to preserve the same attractive physical wholesomeness and the same kindly attitude of soul.

COMING TO CHURCH

A little settlement called Burg is the heart of this little remnant of Lusatia. On Sundays the entire population of the surrounding Wendish world assembles in the church of Burg to worship in the Wendish way and listen to the word of God spoken by Wendish ministers in Wendish words. As soon as the sun is up the congregation begins to arrive. Some worshippers come in boats, some in wagons, but most of them come tramping into town on foot. Many a careful dame we saw trudging along, barefoot, with her Sunday-go-to-meeting shoes in one hand and her prayer-book in the other; and all of those barefooted worshippers paused on the outskirts of the town beside the calm canal and washed their feet, put on their stockings and shoes, and then, neatly shod, walked

solemnly up the main street to the church. By ones and twos
and threes and fours and fives they come, all clad in short full
skirts of black, with full wide *Tücher* of white linen folded in
curious fashion on the head. This gives them all the look of
nuns. In fact, the color of the costume has a certain religious
significance; or rather, this severe costume all in black and
white is that prescribed by custom for church-going on Whit-
sunday and the Sunday after. We are assured that on other
Sundays the same women will be more variously dressed, with
colored skirts and some with colored *Tücher*, wider and gayer
and more picturesque. So we came back another Sunday and
found the costumes far less somber, although the nunlike make-ups
were still in the majority. For two good hours the good people
then shut themselves up in their little church to listen to a sermon
long enough to last them all the week — until they come again to

THE CHURCH AT BURG

KIRCHGANG

Burg, just as their ancestors have been coming Sunday after Sunday these many years. It is so strange to come upon these changeless corners of our changing world, these places where life is lived by the present generation very nearly as it was by the generations of a remote, uneventful, still-persisting past.

The male inhabitants of this little land of other days are just beginning to adopt the cheap and ill-fitting city-made coats and trousers of to-day, but the women are content to follow,

COMING FROM CHURCH

or rather to be held by the immobile fashions that are the same for yesterday as for to-day; and let us pray in the name of all that's quaint and picturesque that no reefs be taken in the *Tücher* of to-morrow, no fullness from the Wendish skirt, no character eliminated from the costume of these good pious dames, who, to my mind, are the best-dressed women in all Germany, because they ignore the horrors devised by modern milliners and the absurdities and extravagances of the changing modern modes, which by the time thay have been Germanized have lost all of the *chic* that saved them from revealing their absurdity in Paris or New York. The city people who come out on Sunday to see the *Kirchgang* here at Burg appear most undistinguished when compared with the native church-goers in their immemorial dress, one costume so like another as to seem almost a uniform.

GOING HOME

Photograph by Wright Kramer.   SPREEWALD REFLECTIONS

A SPREEWALD AVENUE

After church a hasty snack of luncheon at the crowded inn and then away to the most delightful experience of all, the slow meandering cruise along the waterways of the Spreewald. We glide from noon till dark along the swift and sweet canals of an exquisite rural Venice. The Spree is here divided into no fewer than two hundred branches. This network of shallow, silvery streams is spread out over a low-lying land of meadows, woods, and marshes, from one to four miles wide and about thirty-five miles long. The aggregate length of the labyrinthine channels has not been computed but it must be enormous. To traverse all the waterways

ONE OF THE TWO HUNDRED
BRANCHES OF THE SPREE

would be the work of weeks.   There are, however, one or two cruises recognized as offering the highest combination of all the Spreewald charms, and no traveler should fail to make at least one of those little voyages through the woods by water.   The craft employed is called a *Kahn*, a flat-bottomed, scow-like little boat, propelled like a punt by a sturdy boatman who in the language of the profession is known as the *Fährmann*.   He gets five marks (a dollar and a quarter) for a whole

"WIR SITZEN SO FRÖHLICH BEISAMMEN UND HABEN EINANDER SO LIEB"

THE GERMAN BAND AFLOAT

day's punting, or seventy-five cents for the fifteen-mile voyage
that we begin at noon.

He plys his pole gently, the current helps a little, and on we
glide silently — seemingly without effort — hour after hour between
long rows of graceful trees, under frail dainty foot-bridges, past
haystacks, farmers' homes, and pretty little hamlets, every turn of
the canal offering the eye a dainty treat, every moment of the voyage a moment long to be remembered. At intervals we pass
through Venice-like villages with un-Venetian names — Lehde
and Leipe and Eiche and Kannomühle. These villages are
much alike, yet there is no monotony.

At every "street intersection" in Spreewald there is a guide-post
to direct us on our way, to tell us just how far it is by water to
Lübben or to Lübbenau, to point the way to the most neighbor-

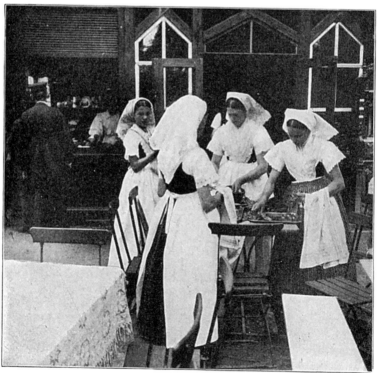

AT THE INN

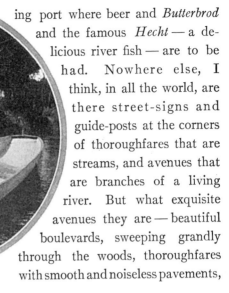

ing port where beer and *Butterbrod* and the famous *Hecht* — a delicious river fish — are to be had. Nowhere else, I think, in all the world, are there street-signs and guide-posts at the corners of thoroughfares that are streams, and avenues that are branches of a living river. But what exquisite avenues they are — beautiful boulevards, sweeping grandly through the woods, thoroughfares with smooth and noiseless pavements,

TOSSING BOUQUETS

A GUIDE-POST AT A WATERY CROSSROADS

streets where no mud lies and no dust flies, streets which become in winter glistening thoroughfares of ice along which the peasants skate from town to town or farm to farm. There are several hundred miles of those fluid streets along which the traveler may glide with the delightful sense of discovering a new earthly paradise, a verdurous Venice with the added charm of a clean and honest population that is at the same time immensely picturesque. Along the way, waiting in native boats moored to the bank, the pretty children stand, ready to toss bouquets of wild flowers into the laps of those

ICH UND MUTTER

who pass. Of course they look for something in return, but the merest trifle pleases, and if you have no change they will smile and stammer *"Danke bestens"* just the same. We met with but one hostile greeting; we were loudly hissed by certain members of a group assembled on the bank to watch the boats go by—but all the members of that group were geese!

To those who ask what all this

BOYS OF BURG

has to do with the city of Berlin I reply that a city's life is not always lived *in* the city; it is lived wherever the people of that city go for recreation. Therefore the Spreewald is as much a part of Berlin as the Brandenburg Gate itself, to which we now return.

The Brandenburg Gate which rises at the western end of Unter-den-Linden is a sandstone imitation of the marble Propy-

THE BRANDENBURG GATE

æa, through which the traveler passes to reach the Parthenon on the Acropolis in Athens. The magnificent Quadriga of Victory, cast in copper, that crowns the noble portal, made a trip to Paris and return about a hundred years ago: Napoleon figuratively drove those four chargers from the banks of the Spree to the banks of the Seine in 1807, intending to place them as symbols of victory upon his arch of triumph in the Place du Carrousel in Paris, but in 1814 the Germans led them back to Berlin, where they now look down on the Pariser Platz and along the "Linden Avenue" from the top of the Brandenburg Gate. Of the five passageways through

THE CHARIOT THAT WENT TO PARIS — AND CAME BACK

the gate, one is reserved exclusively for royal or imperial personages. It is of course the middle one, and though it is not closed by any gate or bar, no German dreams of trying to pass through; but the mischief-loving American is always tempted to try that forbidden way, just to see what would hap-

pen; probably the guard would turn out and salute any one who had the assurance to choose the Kaiser's passageway in coming from the Tiergarten into the Pariser Platz. Appropriately enough the palatial French Embassy is in this Berlinese *Place de Paris* that lies between the gate and the beginning of Unter-den-Linden. The

TOWARD THE TIERGARTEN

palatial British Embassy is in the neighboring Wilhelm Strasse.
Other palatial embassy buildings are to be seen in Berlin — each
one an object of pride, respectively, in the eyes of traveling Frenchmen, Englishmen, Austrians, Russians, Italians, or Spaniards or
subjects of the minor European kingdoms. Even the smaller states

WILHELM STRASSE

of the German Empire — which send their representatives, not
to the Imperial Court, but to the Royal Court of Prussia — provide handsome residences for their envoys. And what of the
United States, the most extravagant if not the richest of great
nations — how does the United States house its Envoy Extraordinary and Ambassador Plenipotentiary? He is not housed
at all by the government that sends him hither! He is provided
with offices upstairs in an old-fashioned four-story building in
Unter-den-Linden. The rent for this dingy suite, to which the

American visitor must climb up a long flight of stairs, is paid by our government; but if the American ambassador desires to emulate the ambassadors of other great nations, or even the ministers of petty states, and entertain socially in a properly appointed house, he is perfectly at liberty to take such a house and do the honors in the name of the United States, *at his own expense.* Fortunately it has so happened of late that the men sent by our government to represent us at the Kaiser's court have been men of great wealth, amply able and willing to bear the cost of "saving the face" of Uncle Sam. The United States should own

THE AMERICAN EMBASSY — OFFICIAL — IS UPSTAIRS—RENT PAID BY THE UNITED STATES

in every foreign capital an embassy or a legation building befitting the dignity of the nation. As a business investment the ownership of centrally located real estate should appeal to our practical legislators, and even if it did not pay in cash it would pay enormous dividends in American prestige abroad, and spare the traveling American many a humiliating comparison.

There has been some question of purchasing the fine mansion in Berlin which at the time of our visit was occupied by the American ambassador but which could not be called the American Embassy save by courtesy — for the enormous rent was paid by the ambassador himself out of his private purse. Let us hope that the penuriousness of our stay-at-home law-makers may not continue much longer to make the maintenance of adequate diplomatic establishments for the American envoys what it is to-day in nearly all the capitals of Europe — a matter of private charity. A little more regard for the social exigencies of the " effete old world "— as we are pleased to call it — would not be undemocratic; we might even excuse ourselves for such a weakness by calling it merely a form of diplomatic " bluff "; at any rate we should never feel the cost, and its effect in Europe would redound greatly to our credit and make impossible the oft-recurring situation, so ridiculous in the eyes of the world, of a great nation — the one whose people spend the most in Europe — being represented at Court by a homeless ambassador, maintaining our diplomatic dignity in a stuffy rented office, able to extend the social courtesies that are a part of his ambassadorial duties, only in the drawing-room of a hotel or in a hired hall. England, for example, provides a palace for her representatives, and in addition to their salaries allows a generous

THE AMERICAN EMBASSY — BY COURTESY — RENT PAID BY THE AMBASSADOR
FROM HIS PRIVATE PURSE

sum annually to defray the cost of the elaborate balls and dinners that are expected — in fact tacitly demanded — of an ambassador or minister.   Some day, no doubt, these words of mine may be read with astonishment, if they are read at all in the future, when the United States shall have had time to attend to what, after all, are the merest details of national policy, for when we

WHERE BISMARCK LIVED

do awake to any need, that need is met and more than met. So, looking beyond the neglectful present, we see in the European capitals of the not distant future a series of diplomatic palaces, simple yet superb, and when the traveler will ask "What is that noble structure, so beautiful, so practical?" the reply will be "That is the Embassy of the United States of America, one of the finest buildings in our city."

Meantime we are strolling under the *Linden* down the finest and most famous avenue toward the finest and most famous

buildings of the city that is both the Prussian capital and the
deutsche Kaiserstadt — metropolis of the German-speaking world.

But all the trees that border the long park-like promenade that
lies between   the driveways

UNTER-DEN-LINDEN

of Unter-den-Linden are not
Linden, or lime trees, for interspersed with
those world-famous *Linden* are hundreds of *Kastanien,* or chest-
nut trees. Very splendid is the long perspective of the promenade
which stretches
straight from the
Brandenburg
Gate and the
Pariser Platz to
the monument of
Frederick the
Great and the
Platz-am-Opern-
haus, two thirds of
a mile distant.
The traveler with

THE MIDDLE OF BERLIN'S CHIEF THROUGHFARE

money in his purse, money he can afford to spend, may safely visit the shops that present attractive fronts to right and left, but he who must avoid the temptations of show-windows may do so easily by "keeping in the middle of the road" between the double lines of lime and chestnut trees, where he may saunter in security along that featureless, monotonous, but at the same time attractive, gravel path, which though it bisects the busy center of Berlin, seems like a peaceful country lane. But the illusion of rurality vanishes suddenly as we reach the end of Unter-den-Linden and see before us the broad open square of the Opera House, flanked by its palaces and monuments. Among the latter, unquestionably the finest, is that of Frederick the Great, a superb work in bronze by Rauch, erected in 1851. The figure of the King on horseback is lifelike in its

FREDERICK THE GREAT

simple dignity. Around the pedestal are smaller figures representing a host of famous personages, — great generals, statesmen,
thinkers, scientists, musicians, poets, dreamers, and doers — each
one of whom added some share of glory or distinction to the reign
of "*der alte Fritz*," as Frederick was lovingly called by his soldiers.

Great Frederick reigned for forty-six
years, from 1740 to 1786. He

AN OPERA HOUSE SURROUNDED
BY PALACES

was a warrior, musician, poet, and philosopher.
He fought with Austria and Russia—in the main successfully,
although his city was twice occupied by foreign troops. Later he
joined Austria and Russia in the partition of poor Poland, a part of
which dismembered land has ever since belonged to Prussia. He
was a patron of the arts. He caused the Royal Opera House to
be erected more than a hundred and seventy years ago. It stands
to-day, the most venerable grand opera house of the entire world.
So marvelously far ahead of its time was it in the beginning, that
to-day, with all the undreamed-of developments in stagecraft
and stage illusion, this opera house designed by Knobelsdorf in

1741 still serves for the adequate presentation of the greater operas in one of the most critical of Continental capitals. The only marring modern touch was applied three years ago, just after the Iroquois disaster in Chicago. Fire escapes, as practical and ample as they are unsightly, were hung like balconies, and broad

THE BERLIN OPERA

out-of-door stairways at four corners of this old-time edifice. Behind the Opera stands another edifice of Frederick's time, the domed church of St. Hedwig, an imitation of the Pantheon at Rome. Fronting upon the same square is the palace, or more properly the home, for it is a home-like palace, of the late Emperor William the Great, grandfather of the Great William of to-day. There at the corner is what the Berliners fondly call the "Historic Window," the window out of which old Emperor William used to look every day to see the guard go by, to take the salute, to salute the flag, and graciously respond to the sincere applause of his enthusiastic, loyal subjects. Since the old Kaiser's death in 1888 the palace has been open to his people, and every day scores of respectful visitors crowd silently into the modest corner room which was in life his favorite apartment. Everything in that room has been preserved just as it was left by the imperial departed. Among other things we see the bust of his imperial consort, the Empress Augusta, who survived him only by two years: the bust of Frederick the Great, whose statue he could look at from the window; portraits of his children and his friends, and scores of those little things that even great men learn to love, — the little things that in time come to play a big part in their daily lives. The window commands a view of the Royal Guard House, head-quarters of the *Königs-Wache*, where the "King's Watch"

FIRE-ESCAPES

watches still before the empty palaces of two dead Emperors, for
the palace of the short-lived Emperor Frederick also faces this
solidest of sentry boxes, which is built in the form of a classic
Roman gate. Guard-mounting takes place daily there at a quarter
before one. The guard is never late, and nothing ever keeps the
crowd away. Rain or shine,
snow or blow,

PALACE OF THE EMPEROR, WILLIAM I

promptly at 12:44 a big
band wakes the echoes of the
Opera Square, and, passing the palace of the vanished Emperor,
the soldiers march with sturdy tread into the railed inclosure at
the *Königs-Wache*, there to go through the brief and snappy
ceremony of relieving guard — always in the presence of a
respectful, interested throng of spectators.

To the left of the Royal Guard House are the buildings of the
University, and to the right the beautiful building called the
Zeughaus with its very pleasing façade, one of the finest architec-
tural features of Berlin. The *Zeughaus*, or Arsenal, now contains
the Military Museum and Hall of Fame of the Prussian Army,

THE KING'S WATCH

where we may study past
campaigns in plans and maps
and models, in uniforms and kits and
camps, and in portraits of the generals and lay-figures of the
men who fought for Prussia and laid the foundations of her
military fame. Everywhere in Berlin we find a tendency to

THE KÖNIGS-WACHE

glorify the war god Mars. The profession of arms is still regarded
by the majority of Prussians as the most honorable and glorious
of all professions. Berlin's streets are always alive with the
officers and soldiers of the present; her parks and squares and

THE ARSENAL

gardens are adorned with bronze and marble effigies of the men
who led the soldiers of the past.

One of the most amusing sights in Berlin is the performance
by a passing regiment or squad of what we incorrectly denominate
the Goose Step, for "goose step" is properly defined as marking
time without making progress. The Germans call it *Parademarsch*.
It is the saluting step of the German army, a peculiar stride
adopted when passing in review before an officer of high rank.
The foot is flung as far forward and as high as possible, with a
vigorous kick-like movement, and then slapped to the pavement
with a spasmodic and yet rhythmic spitefulness. While legs and

feet are making fools of themselves, the body from the hips up must maintain an impassive dignity out of all harmony with the acrobatic activity of the nether limbs. The contrast between the comedy legs and the tragedy torso is to us excruciatingly funny.

THE UNIVERSITY

To reach the Kaiser's palace we must cross the Schloss Brücke, a handsome bridge adorned with works of sculpture that illustrate the life of a warrior. They show us a winged Victory teaching a child the history of heroes; Minerva showing a youth how to employ his weapons; Iris conducting a fallen fighter to Olympus; and similar inspiring incidents to fire the imagination of a military people. Beyond rises the newest of Berlin's great buildings, the Lutheran Cathedral which was begun in 1894. It cost two and a half millions of dollars and is the most conspicuous edifice in town. Artistically it cannot rank with old masterpieces like the Cathedral of Cologne, but it is still a noble structure, worthy of its place in the heart and center of Imperial Berlin. The Royal Palace rises on the right, the beautiful *Lustgarten* lies on the left, and on the far side of that Pleasure Garden stands what is to me the most artistic and imposing building in Berlin. It is the Old Museum, an art temple in the Greek-Ionic style, enshrin-ing a magnificent col-lection of original antiques. The building itself is nobly beau-tiful. Nothing in all

THE NEW DOMKIRCHE FROM THE LUSTGARTEN

architecture is finer, nobler, more impressive than a colossal portico of tall Ionic columns It is to the genius of the architect Schinkel that Berlin owes much of her noble aspect, for Schinkel built as the old Greeks themselves would have built had they lived in our modern day. In front of the grand stairway stands a granite basin, twenty-two feet in diameter. Everybody makes it a point to walk around it and look into it; and little Germans

THE OLD MUSEUM

THE BIG BOWL

have to take a lot of steps to get around it and go to a lot of trouble to get a peep at the inside of it, and although everybody knows that there is nothing in it, still there are always several curious somebodies trying to satisfy their empty curiosity by looking into that big empty bowl. The block from which this bowl

MODERN ART

was cut weighed three
hundred and seven-
ty-five   tons, but
the   bowl itself
weighs only sev-
enty-five tons —
enough, how-
ever, to insure
against its being
stolen in the
night. In this
same classic quar-

ter of Berlin, which is in
fact an island embraced
by two canal-like
branches of the Spree
— just as the Isle de
la Cité in Paris is em-

THE ALTAR OF ZEUS

braced by two branches of the Seine — stand many of the most
famous buildings of the German capital. Behind the Old Museum
is a less imposing art gallery called the New Museum, and behind
it the newer Pergamon Museum opened in 1901, in which we find

THE PERGAMON MARBLES

the splendid Pergamon Marbles adorning the reconstructed altar of Zeus — the largest existing monument of the classic age of Greece. Fragments of this amazing structure were discovered by Carl Humann in 1871 on the site of Pergamon in Asia Minor. It was erected in the year 180 B. C. by King Eumenes II to commemorate his victory over the Gauls. The great frieze

THE NATIONAL PICTURE GALLERY

of the altar, seven and a half feet high and nearly five hundred feet long, portrays in a series of vigorous, heroic reliefs the battle of the gods and giants — a work worthy the hand of Phidias himself.

Other treasure houses of art rise near at hand — the National Picture Gallery in the form of a superb Corinthian temple and the recently completed Emperor Frederick Museum, a superb memorial of the late father of the Kaiser and one of the best equipped art museums in the world, its collection of paintings rivaling in historical completeness that of the National Gallery in London.

On this same island stands the Royal Palace — the *König-liches Schloss* — its various divisions dating from different periods

WILLIAM II

and containing about seven hundred rooms. The most picturesque feature is the little round tower called the "Green Hat" seen from the Kurfürsten Brücke; the most imposing feature is the great gateway in the form of a reproduction of the triumphal arch of Septimius Severus in Rome. To describe the interior would be to repeat the descriptions of nearly any other royal palace of the Continent. To visit in detail the homes of kings and emperors, to tramp through suite after suite of gorgeous apartments, is to learn to value the simple comforts and to appreciate the conveniences of your own little home or your own up-to-date apartment. Royalty seems doomed to dwell in magnificent discomfort; at least the traveler never sees any suggestion of real comfort or convenience in the palaces of Europe. Splendor, magnificence, costliness, yes; but empty splendor, formal magnificence, cold, cheerless

FREDERICK III

costliness; nothing cosy; nothing *intime*; nothing homelike, livable, congenial, — nothing really artistic, because the ostentatious can never be artistic in the full sense of the word. "Art is the best way of doing things" — and there are better ways of building palaces and homes than any royal architect has ever yet devised.

THE ROYAL PALACE AND THE KURFÜRSTEN-BRÜCKE

Costliness and ostentation characterize also the Emperor William Memorial, an elaborate work in bronze and marble that rises between the Schloss and the Spree. It was unveiled on March 22, 1897, the hundredth anniversary of the old Emperor's birthday. It cost one million dollars, and to provide space for it the River Spree was narrowed many feet. A long Ionic colonnade curves round the ornate pedestal, which is adorned with so many and such fearful and menacing beasts of prey that some facetious Berlinese refer to this grandiose conception as "William in the Lion's

Den"! Still as a monument it is imposing. We see the noble form of the Emperor astride his favorite charger, Hippocrates, led by a female figure bearing the olive branch of peace. Around the pedestal winged victories are poised; between them are reliefs that illustrate the blessings of Peace, and the horrors of War.

THE KAISER AND HIS STAFF

Seated upon the steps, a warrior of colossal size, and at the corners roaring lions trampling on trophies and guarding the wreck of battlefields. Whether the monument glorifies Peace or War it is not easy to determine. The Kaiser who erected it in memory of his imperial ancestor declares himself both the Champion of Peace and the War Lord of the German people. For more than twenty years he has reigned over them as a soldier, and given them the blessings born of peace; for more than twenty years his chief task has been the development of the system of the military training, thanks to which Germany could mobilize on a moment's

PARADEMARSCH!

notice five or six million perfectly trained
fighting men — to preserve the peace of
Europe. The German Kaiser holds in his
grasp the mightiest instrument of war ever
forged by any nation, the biggest and most
perfect   fighting machine the world
has ever seen — the German
army — the most potent
guarantee of peace, the
most portentous agent of
destruction in the modern
world. Germany stands to-
day secure in her preparedness.

Of all great nations she is without
question the most unfavorably located —
her landward frontiers exposed to the
attack of old-time enemies, her frontage
on the seas not continuous, for Denmark
lies between her western and her
northern coasts, and were it

THE WAR-LORD

not for the Kiel Canal her ships would have to steam around the north end of the Danish peninsula to get from Kiel or Lübeck to Hamburg or Bremen. The area of the Empire is comparatively small, only a little more than two hundred thousand square miles; our State of Texas is larger by nearly sixty thousand square miles than the entire territory of United Germany. The population of the Empire numbers to-day about sixty-two millions,— twice the population of the same regions sixty years ago. At one time, just after the Thirty Years War, Germany found herself nearly depopulated, only about four million inhabitants having survived that long period of strife, famine, and suffering. Real poverty reigned in Germany until the Franco-Prussian War. Since 1870 Germany has grown rich — has moved more rapidly along the road of progress and prosperity than any other

AT THE IMPERIAL GATE

European nation. Of her enormous present population more than two thirds dwell in the towns and cities, which are almost without exception centers of great industrial activity. From the position of a poverty-stricken and war-ravaged agricultural nation, Germany has advanced to that of a rich,

peace-preserving industrial nation whose little label "*Made* WAR TROPHIES *in Germany*" has made its triumphant way around the world, upsetting the economic equilibrium of many a manufacturing community. All this amazing progress along the paths of peace has been made to the sound of military music, but at the same time the rattle of the loom has been heard above the clank of the saber, the racket of the steel riveters above the roar of rifle practice, and the mental processes of the German master-minds in chemistry and in all the scientific industries have done more for Germany than all the manœuvers of her army or the strategic cruises of her fleets. Has Germany succeeded because of her preparedness for war, or has she succeeded in spite of it? Her military preëminence and her increasing naval prominence cost her people dear, for in addition to the enormous expenditures made by the government for the equipment and maintenance of her great army and navy there must be added the enormous total made up of the modest sums provided by devoted families for the support of the young men during their period of service in the ranks or on the seas.

It is notorious that an officer cannot live upon his pay alone; and the same is practically true of the men, for their pay is not sufficient, and it must be supplemented by gifts of money from the loved ones at home. Thus the German people support their soldiers and their sailors, not only indirectly through taxation, but directly by sending, from time to time, the little sums that make life possible for a self-respecting wearer of the Kaiser's uniform. Out of their earnings, the millions of workers must pay for the clothing and the food and drink of the hundreds of thousands of those prospective defenders of the Fatherland.

THE ARMY . . . AND THE PEOPLE

But is all that crushing military burden necessary? This is the question asked by the "plain people," the tax-payers, as they stand in the presence of the great War Giant they have bred and reared and which they now have to feed and clothe and keep supplied with powder and with steel. Is this monstrous thing of blood and discipline — this German army — worth what it costs the people in gold, in labor, and in sacrifice? This is the question which Humanity is asking. The War Lord has his answer ready. His people may find yet another. Let us hope that the answer will not be one that will shake the foundations of civilization, that the guiding hand of him who sits upon the German throne and the sturdy common-sense of those who call him Kaiser, may so wisely control this unparalleled incarnation of military power — this army of the Fatherland — that it may never, like the monster made by Frankenstein, become a thing that even its creator cannot master.

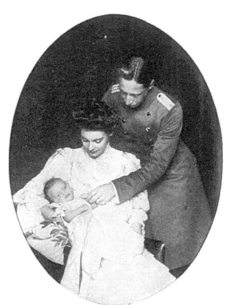

THE FUTURE

FURTHER READING

Baedeker's *Germany* (1995) and Eugene Fodor's *Germany* (1995) each contain contemporary descriptions of Hamburg and Berlin, the two major cities described by Holmes in his 1907 travelogue. It is interesting to compare descriptions of these cities today with what Holmes wrote 90 years ago.

Anyone who wishes to find out about the major events and personalities of Europe between 1875 and 1914 should read Eric Hobsbawn's *The Age of Empire: 1875-1914* (1989). Other interesting books on the period include *Europe 1815-1914* by Gordon Craig; James Joll's *Europe Since 1870;* and *A Survey of European Civilization* (Vol. II, from 1660), by Wallace K. Ferguson and Geoffrey Brown. See also: Barbara Tuchman, *The Proud Tower* (1966); Edward R. Tannenbaum, *1900: The Generation Before the Great War* (1976); and *War by Timetable: How the First World War Began* (1969), *The Struggle for Mastery in Europe, 1848-1918* (1971), and *The Last of Old Europe: A Grand Tour* (1976), by A. J. P. Taylor.

—Dr. Fred L. Israel

CONTRIBUTORS

General Editor FRED L. ISRAEL is an award-winning historian. He received the Scribe's Award from the American Bar Association for his work on the Chelsea House series *The Justices of the United States Supreme Court.* A specialist in American history, he was general editor for Chelsea's *1897 Sears Roebuck Catalog.* Dr. Israel has also worked in association with Arthur M. Schlesinger, jr. on many projects, including *The History of U.S. Presidential Elections* and *The History of U.S. Political Parties.* He is senior consulting editor on the Chelsea House series *Looking into the Past: People, Places, and Customs,* which examines past traditions, customs, and cultures of various nations.

Senior Consulting Editor ARTHUR M. SCHLESINGER, JR. is the preeminent American historian of our time. He won the Pulitzer Prize for his book *The Age of Jackson* (1945), and again for *A Thousand Days* (1965). This chronicle of the Kennedy Administration also won a National Book Award. He has written many other books, including a multi-volume series, *The Age of Roosevelt.* Professor Schlesinger is the Albert Schweitzer Professor of Humanities at the City University of New York, and has been involved in several other Chelsea House projects, including the *American Statesmen* series of biographies on the most prominent figures of early American history.

IRVING WALLACE (1916-1990), whose essay on Burton Holmes is reprinted in the forward to The World 100 Years Ago, is one of the most widely read authors in the world. His books have sold over 200 million copies, and his best-sellers include *The Chapman Report, The Prize, The Man, The Word, The Second Lady,* and *The Miracle.*

INDEX